£6

The
CHRISTIAN
HERO

A Sketch of the Life of
ROBERT ANNAN

Robert Annan (1834-1867)

The
CHRISTIAN
HERO

A Sketch of the Life of
ROBERT ANNAN

JOHN MACPHERSON

Kingsley Press
Shoals, Indiana

The Christian Hero:
A Sketch of the Life of Robert Annan

PUBLISHED BY KINGSLEY PRESS
PO Box 973
Shoals, IN 47581
USA

Tel. (800) 971-7985
www.kingsleypress.com
E-mail: sales@kingsleypress.com

ISBN: 978-1-937428-33-4

First published 1867

First Kingsley Press edition 2013

Contents

Preface

There is an old story, the substance of which is this: from sin to grace, and from grace to glory. The story has its variations of person, place, time, and circumstance; but the outcome of it is ever the same: salvation is of the Lord. The first part is known to all, for it tells of sin. The second part is stranger than fiction, for it tells of grace. The first part is this: a sinner buckles on his armour, flings down his challenges to the Almighty, advances to battle against Him, is emboldened by sundry successes, finds a secret pleasure in fighting against so great odds, and laughs at the thunderbolts of heaven. In the second part matters are reversed. The Almighty advances against the sinner, shoots him through and through with sharp arrows, but they are arrows of light; heaps coals of fire upon his head, but the fire is love; and obtains a victory with the shedding of no blood but that of the Conqueror. The upshot strangely enough is this: the sinner takes up arms and begins to fight in deadly earnest against himself. There is now a solemn league and covenant between the Saviour and the saved one, and they are henceforth devoted friends.

The following narrative is that same story of sin and salvation. It is, I need hardly say, no finely-spun fiction, but plain, genuine fact. Though far too hurriedly written—written as it has been in weary hours snatched from the incessant demands of a laborious town ministry, it is earnestly commended to the grace of God and the sympathies of all who pray, "Thy kingdom come!"

Dundee

Publisher's Foreword

As of two months ago, I had never heard of Robert Annan of Dundee. The reading of this biography in preparation for republication has been an unforgettable experience. For its size, it is easily one of the most powerful Christian biographies I've ever read.

I was introduced to the book by a friend, Mona Leiter, whose husband Charles pastors Lake Road Chapel in Kirksville, Missouri (lakeroadchapel.org). She told me the book is exceedingly rare and encouraged me to think about republishing it. I would like to express my thanks to her for the suggestion and for her encouragement throughout the preparation of the book for the press, as well as supplying the photo of the "eternity stone" that appears on page 94. I would also like to express sincere thanks to Mike Cleary for scanning and emailing the text of the book to me, and also Linda Sutton and Jill Belling for volunteering their proofreading skills.

Robert Annan's transformation by the grace of God from a life of reckless debauchery to one of exemplary holiness and almost unbelievable endeavors in seeking to win lost souls to Christ easily parallels that of more widely known examples, such as John Newton, Billy Bray and many others. His story deserves to be read and learned from. May this small volume serve as a reminder to many that what God did for Robert Annan of Dundee in the 19th century he can do for anyone, anywhere, and in any generation.

The text found here is complete and unabridged, with only minimal editing to update punctuation for easier reading.

Edward Cook
June, 2013

1

Wandering

All we like sheep have gone astray; we have turned every one to his own way; and the Lord hath laid on Him the iniquity of us all (Isaiah 53:6).

> I was a wandering sheep,
>   I did not love the fold;
> I did not love the Shepherd's voice,
>   I would not be controlled.
>
> I was a wayward child,
>   I did not love my home,
> I did not love my Father's voice,
>   I loved afar to roam.

Robert Annan was born at Hilltown, Dundee, on the 5th of October, 1834. He was the son of respectable parents, who sent him when a child to school. The boy was fonder of play than of books; and often, instead of striving to master his lessons, he was contending with his fists. Active even to restlessness, he would rise before the break of day and hie to the fields for sport. To secure his early awaking he would hang out at his bedroom window a string, one end of which was fastened to his ankle; at early morn, ere yet anyone in the house was astir, his companions came and pulled the string, and the sleeper arose. Fearless and fond of daring, he would plunge into the water—river or sea—wherever and whenever he found an opportunity. He would bathe in time of frost or snow, and quickly became an accomplished and courageous swimmer. He attained such ease and power in the water that he was named "The Water-Dog," and this mastery he successfully turned to one of the noblest uses, that of saving human life.

As he grew up, the native wildness of his character developed itself with alarming rapidity. He became reckless, wayward, ungovernable, and fierce. Neither his master nor his parents could hold him in check. His passionate and lawless nature would frequently break through all bounds, and spend its force in terrible doings, like the foaming billows upon the seashore. Yet amidst all this impetuosity and violence of character, there was something gallant and chivalrous in the man—he was kind-hearted and generous to a fault.

At the age of fourteen he was apprenticed to a merchant as clerk; but he would not settle at the desk, and after his time had expired he served his father as a mason. Ere this he had begun to frequent the tavern, and speedily became the ringleader in drinking, swearing, fighting, and kindred vices, till at last he found himself in prison, where he lay for three months. Sobriety and sense returned with solitude, and as he lay in his cell he resolved to amend his ways. Weary of his involuntary confinement, he prayed to God for release, and foolishly imagined that the sincerity of his heart and the goodness of his resolutions were so meritorious in the sight of God that an angel might be sent, as in the case of Peter, to deliver him out of prison. No angel came, save the angel of justice; at the end of three months Robert was free. But his good resolutions, like the green withes with which Samson was bound, vanished in the presence of the first temptation. He seemed now to be hopelessly gone in folly. His father gave him a sum of money and sent him to America, where, instead of recovering himself, as he had promised, and his friends expected, he made a fresh start in the devil's service, and played the part of the prodigal son in the far country. Although he had suffered shipwreck on his way to the New World, and escaped death as by a hair's-breadth, he no sooner set foot on land than he plunged headlong into sin, faster even than before. In his utter abandonment, one night, in a freak of mad indifference—or of wild despair—he threw himself across a railway and slept, escaping destruction only by some miracle of God's providence.

His money was now spent and his clothes worn out. After sundry adventures he passed from the States into Canada, and during the rigours of winter he went about shivering with cold and weak through hunger and want, searching for employment, but in vain. Here he met a man who had pity on the forlorn wanderer and took him to his house. It happened that this man subsisted by rearing swine, and for a time Robert literally acted the part of the prodigal son and assisted his host in feeding the swine. Finding no suitable employment, Robert enlisted in the 100th Regiment, which shortly afterwards went to England and encamped at Aldershot.

In the army he met with Christian friends who took a kind interest in his welfare, tendered him good advice, and prayed and laboured for his salvation. Wherever he went during his unconverted days, as he used to tell, he was continually met and followed by the prayers and loving offices of earnest Christians. This he attributed to the sovereign grace of God, which pursued him from hill to valley, till at length the Good Shepherd laid the wandering sheep upon His shoulders and brought him back to the fold. It may here be mentioned that his godly friends in the army continued to pray for him long after he had forsaken them, plunged anew into folly, and disappeared; nor did they cease their intercession until they heard of his conversion.

Let those who are praying for the unconverted be encouraged to hope and wait. Is it not written: "Ask Me of things to come concerning My sons, and concerning the work of My hands command ye Me" (Isa. 45:11)?

But to return. For a short season the stern restraints of the service, together with the influence of Christian fellow-soldiers and others, wrought some external reformation on Robert; and being now employed as a teacher, he began to respect himself and be useful to others. Suddenly, however, one day the old spirit of evil obtained the ascendancy, and he deserted. Disguised in the cast-off clothes of a peasant, with a tattered jacket, a boot on one foot and a shoe on the other, he pursued his way across fields and through hedges towards London, which he reached in a miserable plight. His liberty brought him small pleasure, for he knew not what to do or where to go. Seeing a company of marines, he went and enlisted in the naval service for the sake of the bounty, on which he made merry and managed for a day or two to forget his misery. This did not last long. He had deserted because his regiment had been ordered to Gibraltar, and to be stationed on the rock he imagined would prove to him sheer imprisonment. And now his ship, the Edgar, was sent to that very place. In this he marked the hand of that God whom he was constantly striving, but in vain, to forget. From the deck of the Edgar he could see his old comrades of the 100th Regiment on the Rock. He became extremely unhappy. Might they not discover that Robert Mackie (he had now assumed his mother's patronymic) was none other than Robert Annan the deserter? Every time he saw a red-coat he fancied he was about to be seized. Conscience began to upbraid him, till at length he was constrained by the voice within to give himself up as a deserter.

After suffering punishment for his offences, he again resolved to turn over a new leaf, and now thought he had done with sin for ever. In this spirit he wrote to his parents, who procured his discharge, and Robert returned to his father's house, seemingly a sadder and a wiser man. One truth he well knew; in one text of Scripture he believed: "The way of transgressors is hard" (Prov. 13:15).

2

Returning

Him that cometh to Me I will in no wise cast out (John 6:37).

Jesus sought me when a stranger,
     Wandering from the fold of God;
He, to save my soul from danger,
     Interposed His precious blood.

Oh, to grace how great a debtor
     Daily I'm constrained to be!
Let that grace, Lord, like a fetter,
     Bind my wandering heart to Thee.

As yet Robert Annan knew only his own righteousness and strength. He had abandoned the tavern, the theatre, and his old companions. He became proud of his newly-begun moralities and began to reckon himself "as good as there was any use for." When the doctrine of the new birth was discussed, he poured contempt upon the very idea of being born again, and went the length of saying that the narrative of our Lord's life was got up by designing men. A few days after this discussion, he went, in the strength of his new reformation, to a public house to fetch away from the scene of temptation a friend of his own. His friend signified his willingness to go if Robert would consent to drink a single glass. He did so; but immediately the desire to drink another, and remain with the company, took possession of him. The rest

I need not tell: a drunken carousal followed. Next morning he looked around upon the total wreck of his resolutions, his reforms, and his hopes. The dog had returned to his vomit. He was filled with confusion and alarm. "What?" he said to himself. "Has it come to this again? Am I past all redemption? Surely I have sold myself to the devil! What shall I do?" Chagrin at the failure of his good intentions and solemn vows confounded his pride and stung him to the quick. The gall and wormwood of remorse embittered his soul, and a melancholy feeling of hopelessness began to possess him.

That night he was so far humbled as to go to a revival meeting—one of a series of meetings then being held in the Kinnaird Hall. In those days (1860–61) the Spirit of God was working very gloriously in the town of Dundee and throughout the land. Many were awakened from the deadly sleep of sin and self-righteousness, and many were seeking and finding the Lord, some of whom have since finished their course and gone to be with Jesus; but the greater number remain and are walking with God to this day. The meeting was addressed by ministers of the town and by brethren from a distance, amongst whom were Mr. George Campbell of Free North Church, Aberdeen, and Mr. Duncan Matheson, men of God who have been signally owned of the great Master in the conversion of many souls. In after-years he spoke with gratitude of the blessing he received that night through Mr. Campbell and the other speakers. During the meeting Robert felt as if he were a target for every shooter; the arrows of conviction stuck fast in his conscience; eternal realities burst upon his view, and the powerful strivings of the Holy Spirit baffled his endeavours to maintain a sullen reserve.

At the close of the meeting he felt disposed to join the company of weeping enquirers, but shame prevented him.

As he stood upon the doorsteps a young man exhorted him to decide, and then bade him good-night, saying, "We shall meet at the judgment seat." "The judgment seat," repeated the trembling sinner to himself; "yes, yes, it is true I must go there."

Every old truth seemed now to flash new light into his soul. Just as he was going to enter the enquiry meeting, the hall door was closed in his face, and he reeled down the steps, exclaiming, "Great God, am I shut out of salvation for ever?" Away he went to the house of a friend, who assured him he might find an entrance into the hall by another door. In breathless haste he returned to seek the door, but in vain. These are small matters; but to an awakened soul such things seem to speak with the voice of God.

At the midnight hour he entered my room and stood before me, his eyes wild and red with excitement and his countenance black and terrible. His whole body, a frame of iron, shook and quivered. Knowing something of the man, I feared he was about to lay hands upon me and take vengeance for some words of reproof. Very different was the case. Robert had now no blows but for himself, and with words of keen and cutting self-condemnation he asked the question of questions, "What must I do to be saved?" I pointed him to the Lamb of God, but in vain; Robert went away as he came, smiting on his breast and calling aloud for mercy.

In his wretchedness he resolved to retire to the top of the Law—a hill which rises almost from the banks of the Tay and overlooks Dundee—and spend the night in solitude and prayer. But although a child could find its way to the summit, and he had been familiar with the hill and its environs from infancy, Robert failed to reach the sought-for solitude. "I could see no hill," he afterwards said to me; "the mountain of my sin rose before my eyes, and the wrath of God like a mist blinded me." A voice then seemed to say, "Go to Camperdown woods, where you used to desecrate the Lord's Day, and end your existence." As he pondered this suggestion, he said to himself, "If I do so, what next?" He shuddered at the thought, and turned his back on Camperdown woods. Then the voice said, "Go to Reres hill, where you used to break the Sabbath, and pray to God on the spot where you sinned, and He will forgive you."

It appears to be a common device of Satan's either to drive to despair or draw into false peace. If a man utterly despairs he may be easily induced to destroy himself; if not, the rebound from despair will be to some desperate penance and lying trust.

Robert did not go to Reres hill to do penance; but returning home he went to a hay loft, where during the night and all next day, for the space of thirteen hours, he lay on his face before God, and with agonizing cries pleaded for mercy. Strange indeed was the scene enacted in that hay loft. Too familiar had that sinner been with deeds of violence and blood; but the hay loft struggle was more terrible than any he had ever passed through. Surely the angels were looking down upon that once hardened blasphemer and exclaiming: "Behold, he prayeth!" Light and darkness were in conflict; grace and sin were striving for the mastery; Christ and the devil contended for that soul; while heaven and hell seemed to hold their breath in expectation of the issue.

Alarmed at his absence, his parents and sister sought him next day, and discovering him by hearing his groanings in the hay loft, induced him to enter the house; but he could neither eat, drink, nor sleep; and for three days the conflict went on, his darkness the while deepening, his anguish growing more keen, and his burden more intolerable, as he lay bemoaning himself and crying with a piteous voice for help.

In company with my friend Mr. Campbell, I went to see him and found him in a darkened room, alone and upon his knees, panting and pleading for mercy like one who had not five minutes to live. Like many an awakened sinner, he was evidently seeking peace with God by trying to pray himself into a better state of heart instead of looking out to Jesus as "THE LORD OUR RIGHTEOUSNESS."

"Robert," said we to him, "you are looking for a sign from heaven. You think if you heard a voice assuring you of salvation, or felt some strange thing within you, you would then believe and rest on Jesus. God gives you His word; why will you not rest on *that*? The gospel of Christ 'is the power of God unto salvation to every one that believeth.' Believe, and it will be the power of God unto salvation to you. 'Believe on the Lord Jesus Christ, and thou shalt be saved.' Jesus says, 'Him that cometh to Me I will in no wise cast out.'"

Robert confessed that he had been seeking a sign from heaven; and had in fact, but a little before we entered, listened in the hope of hearing a voice say, "Robert, your sins are all forgiven." It is difficult to convince an unconvinced sinner of sin, and it is equally hard to convince a convinced sinner of salvation through the blood of the Lamb. But this is the work of the Holy Spirit. Robert was near the kingdom, but he did not at that hour enter in. We left him where we found him, at the mercy seat. At the end of three days he was enabled to lay hold upon the word of Jesus, "Him that cometh to Me I will in no wise cast out" (John 6:37). There he cast anchor, and although in after-years he encountered many a storm, no blast was ever able to drive him from his moorings. He was safe on the Rock.

Thus the grace of God obtained a victory over this stout-hearted sinner. And the victory was complete. The man of iron nature became soft and impressible as melted wax. His fierce, turbulent, and ungovernable passions were hushed into a settled calm; the lion had become a lamb. His proud, fighting, desperate temper was changed to meekness; and a little child could lead him. The mainspring of sin in his heart was broken. What pains and penalties, military and naval discipline, imprisonments, bonds and brands, hunger and thirst, poverty and nakedness, good resolutions and solemn vows, moral reform and remorse, the labours and prayers of the godly, the tears and entreaties of parents, narrow escapes from death and the smitings of God's providence, had utterly failed to effect, was accomplished as in a moment by the power of the Holy Ghost. The fierce wind, the earthquake, and the fire assailed this stronghold of Satan in vain; but when the still small voice of pardon, bringing peace, stole in upon the rebel's ear, immediately the citadel was won. Down went the proud flag of rebellion, with its mottoes: Sin, Self-will, Self-trust, Independence of God; and up went the banner of Jesus and Salvation, and on the banner was written "LOVE." Old things had now passed away and all things were become new. Rejoicing in the efficacy of the blood of Jesus, he could now sing:

> My faith looks up to Thee,
> Thou Lamb of Calvary,
> 　　　Saviour divine!
> Now hear me while I pray,
> Take all my guilt away,
> Oh, let me from this day
> 　　　Be wholly Thine.

May Thy rich, grace impart
Strength to my fainting heart,
    My zeal inspire:
As Thou hast died for me,
Oh, may my love to Thee,
Pure, warm, and changeless be,
    A living fire.

When life's dark maze I tread,
And griefs around me spread,
    Be Thou my guide;
Bid darkness turn to day,
Wipe sorrow's tears away,
Nor let me ever stray
    From Thee aside.

When ends life's transient dream,
When death's cold, sullen stream
    Shall o'er me roll,
Blest Saviour, then in love,
Fear and distrust remove;
Oh, bear me safe above—
    A ransomed soul!

Thus did Robert Annan now sing; so did he teach others to sing; and the same song of salvation through the blood of the Lamb is he singing even now amidst that great congregation whose praises never cease.

And how many weary souls have rested on that same word of Christ's: "Him that cometh to Me I will in no wise cast out." In the faith of it great minds and weak intellects have launched out into eternity. Bishop Butler, when dying, expressed his fears that the Lord would not receive him. His chaplain reminded him that Jesus had said, "Him that cometh to Me I will in no wise cast out," to which the bishop replied, "I never saw that before." And the great thinker, with the simplicity of a child, pillowed his head upon the promise, and fell asleep.

"How did you obtain deliverance?" I asked of one who would be reckoned amongst Paul's "weak things." "Ah, sir," was the reply, "the more I struggled, the deeper I sank in the mire, till at length I got deliverance through the smallest word in the Bible. In my extremity this promise came to my heart with power, 'Him that cometh to Me I will in no wise cast out'; and I got relief to my soul, not so much from what He said as from seeing who said it. Ah, sir, that's a glorious 'I.'" The simple woman had seen the glory of the only begotten of the Father, full of grace and truth, and she at once rested on Jesus. "And many a precious 'I,'" she added, with the tears streaming down her cheeks, "have I found in the Bible since that time."

Reader, are you seeking salvation? By which of the ways do you seek it—by the way of works or by grace? The way of works is the more popular way, but it will take you to all eternity to find salvation in that way. By God's method, by grace simple and pure, you may obtain salvation even this very day.

> There is life for a look at the crucified One,
>   There is life at this moment for thee:
> Then look, sinner, look unto Him and be saved—
>   Unto Him who was nailed to the tree.

You may say this is a strong way of speaking. Yes, but it is true. This is a question of righteousness. Now, there is man's righteousness and there is God's righteousness. By the righteousness of man shall no flesh be justified (Rom. 3:20). Men go about in a hundred ways to establish their own righteousness. "Go to," says Old Self, "and let us establish a claim on God and so secure salvation." So men set up a rival cross beside that of Calvary; and when the voice of incarnate God cries, "It is finished," the rival worker, Old Self, replies, "Nay, it is not finished. Stay till I have done my part; it cannot be finished without me." This is what you do when you labour to do something, or bring something, or wait to feel something, or be something, in order to obtain mercy unto salvation. What shall I do?—Nothing. What shall I bring?—Nothing. What shall I suffer?—Nothing. What shall I feel?—Nothing. What shall I be?—Nothing; nothing but what you are, a poor helpless sinner at the feet of the Saviour; and the moment you, a sinner, and nothing but a sinner, with your bad heart and all your sins upon you, lay hold with that black sinful hand of yours on the outstretched hand of Jesus as "the Lord our Righteousness," that moment you are saved. Does something in your heart object, saying, "You make salvation too cheap and easy"? That is your pride; it is Old Self that so speaks. But what saith the Lord? "Believe on the Lord Jesus Christ, and thou shalt be saved" (Acts 16:31). "To him that worketh not, but believeth on Him that justifieth the ungodly, his faith is counted for righteousness" (Rom. 4:5). "He that believeth on the Son hath everlasting life" (John 3:36).

3

Working in the Vineyard

Son, go work today in my vineyard (Matthew 21:28).

> E'er since by faith I saw the stream
> Thy flowing wounds supply,
> Redeeming love has been my theme,
> And shall be till I die.

In every true convert's heart there is a desire, often intensely fervent, to bring others to Jesus. He must speak of what he knows; he must tell what he has found. He would fain share his joy with everyone he meets. Here is the Messiah! Andrew tells Peter, and Philip tells Nathanael. This desire is born of the Holy Ghost. It is love; and to quench it, therefore, is great wickedness. It is extreme folly on the part of any believer, and a great loss to his own soul, and it may be also a grievous loss to the souls of others, if from carnal policy, a spurious humility, or the fear of man, he suffers the desire to win souls, and to extend by personal effort the kingdom of God, to languish and die. No Christian ever attains to eminent grace who does not learn to be useful. It is not possible to have bowels of compassion, or to walk in the footsteps of Jesus, and behold with cold indifference the great crowd of the unsaved sweeping past to hell. "Once on crossing a lake," said a venerable Christian, "a sudden squall upset our boat and threw us all into the water. I forgot everything in the world and thought only of my life. I forgot about everyone else; I thought only of myself. After a desperate struggle I reached the shore; and no sooner had I wiped the water from my eyes than I remembered my poor companions who were still in the deep water and at once rushed in to help them." So the man who but the other day escaped, as by a miracle of grace, eternal death, will feel for those who are perishing, and hasten to their rescue. "Ye are My witnesses," saith the Lord; and a witness needs not talent or influence or learning or eloquence: it is only required of a witness that he speak the truth. The truth as it is in Jesus is a talent possessed by every true believer, and he is not at liberty to tie it in a napkin or hide it in the earth.

Robert Annan began to employ his talent in the Master's service on the very day of his conversion. "Give me some tracts," he said, after telling me how he had found salvation through the blood of the Lamb. "I wish to do something for Christ." That night he took his stand at the door of a hall in which a certain skeptic (since converted to Christ) was to lecture against the religion of Jesus and the revelation of God, and distributed his tracts amongst those who entered, fearing not to testify for the truth; whilst his very face, radiant with the joy of salvation, preached the gospel to all who knew him. The change in his spirit, character, and life was so marked that all the people took knowledge of him that he had been with Jesus. The newly-kindled light of grace he could not conceal, and if he could have concealed it he would not have done so. He was henceforth an epistle of Christ, which even men of the world could read and understand. And such was the force of his character and the power of God in its sanctification that he seemed to pass almost at once from eminence in sin to eminence in holiness and grace.

On the second night after his conversion he was asked to speak at a meeting. He stood up at once and told the audience what the Lord had done for his soul; and henceforth until the day of his death, a period of seven years, Robert threw all his heart and soul into the work of God. He had a passion for saving souls, and the Lord gave him great success. He had little knowledge and less tact to begin with; but he served a Master who overlooks the faults of his servants and blesses their good intentions. His voice was harsh, but it was strong; his manner was rough, but it was manly; his matter was occasionally crude, but it was ever downright truth; his earnestness was vehement and terrible, but it was genuine and sincere; and his aim, though sometimes misdirected, was always noble and Christlike, for he aimed at the glory of God in the salvation of souls.

We ought not to forget that in Christ's band there are many instruments of various sorts. To Robert was given a ram's horn; and many a strong blast did he blow, as during his week of years he walked round and round the walls of Jericho. Nervous people put their fingers in their ears, for the ram's horn was not sweetly musical or according to science; but Robert went on blowing. Men of Jericho laughed and mocked; Robert went on and "spared not." Some cursed and swore; the ram's horn waxed louder and louder. "He will do more harm than good," said the timid folks; but Robert, having no idea of timidity on a field of battle, thought only of obeying his Captain's order, and went on as before. "He may go on blowing till doomsday," said all Jericho; "he will make nothing of it." But Robert, feeling certain that doomsday was coming, went on sounding the ram's horn as loudly as if he had been ordained to trumpet in the final judgment. And certain it is that, ere he had gone his last round and blown his last blast, great breaches were made in the walls, and great towers of Jericho had fallen, as even the men of Jericho themselves must acknowledge.

A band of young men, whose hearts God had touched during the great awakening, formed themselves into a little Evangelistic Association. They met weekly for prayer, study of the Word, spiritual conference, and laying out their plans of usefulness. Their great object, next to mutual improvement and encouragement in the ways of God, was to visit the sick and dying, hold meetings for prayer and exhortation in destitute localities, and, in short, to carry the good news of salvation to the ignorant, the careless, and the outcast. Some of those young men are still engaged in the same good work; some have since prepared for the regular ministry of the gospel; and some are gone to be with the Lord. Robert, shortly after his conversion, joined the society of the young men and soon became their president. His extraordinary zeal inflamed that of his brethren to the highest pitch; and the blessing of God signally attended their labours. About this time he made the following private jottings:

1. I am not what I once was; but by the grace of God I am what I am, an empty sinner depending on Christ, a full and present Saviour.

2. My creed is this: Ruin by the Fall; Redemption by the Cross; and Regeneration by the Holy Spirit.

3. My knowledge of Scripture is small, for it is not long since I was plucked as a brand from the fire; but I am hungering to know more, and God by His Holy Spirit will teach me the truths contained in His glorious gospel. I feel myself nothing, and can do nothing; but I go forward looking up to Him who has said, "Open thy mouth wide, and I will fill it" (Psa. 81:10).

4. I have seriously weighed the difficulties I must meet in the service of God; and in His strength I will bear the cross which every faithful follower of Jesus has borne. This has been a matter of earnest prayer, and I firmly believe that God is with me. I see nothing before me but to fight the Lord's battles; but leaning on His arm I shall hold up the banner of the cross and hope to obtain a humble place in His service.

Robert was at this time employed as a mason. At his work he stood up for his Saviour, and often fearlessly rebuked sin, testifying at the same time to the grace of God. His evenings were spent in street preaching or in meetings within doors, whilst he frequently spent whole nights in secret prayer. He went often to the country to speak of Jesus, and for this end took long journeys at night after a hard day's toil. To many a rural parish and many a village did he go with his unvarnished story about saving grace. And if his grammar, his rhetoric, and his theology were not always of the best, the man himself was a more powerful sermon than many a polished discourse. Instant in season and out of season, he created opportunities of usefulness where no opportunity presented itself; his unbounded zeal and dauntless bearing always cleared the way.

Sometimes he managed to save as much of his wages as furnished him with means for a fortnight's evangelistic tour. One of the first places he visited in this way was the county of Fife, where his labours were blessed to a considerable number of souls. At the first meeting he began by saying, "You remember, friends, that when I was last here I sang 'Lord Lovel,' acted the part of a fool, and did my best to entertain you with vanity. I have come on a different errand this time, and will sing to you other songs. I was then employed in the devil's service, but now I am in the service of Christ. At that time I was making merry on the way to hell, and I was helping to make you merry in the same way; but now I am happy in Jesus and on the road to heaven, and I have come to try and persuade you to go with me to glory." He went on to speak from the text, "The love of Christ constraineth me." His audiences were thunderstruck. The word was with great power. Some did not know what to think about this new style of things, but others were humbled at the feet of Jesus. And the fruits remain to this day. He held a great many meetings at different places and was much encouraged by the results.

In 1862 our street preacher married, and about the same period went to labour as a missionary in connection with the

Northeast Coast Mission, an institution which, under the energetic and faithful superintendence of Mr. Donald Ross, has been largely instrumental in reviving and fostering the work of God along a vast extent of our northern shores. He was stationed at Stonehaven, and for a good many months prosecuted his mission there and in the neighbouring villages. Here he met with much to discourage him. The people did not want to hear about the necessity of being born again. Many were grossly carnal and some foully blasphemous. Not contented with venting their spleen by scoffing at the simple-hearted man of God, some laid violent hands upon him. Though much tried, he bore the ill-usage meekly, and often wrestled in prayer for a blessing. Seeing no fruit of his labour, he began to fear that God was not with him. This led to humiliation and prayer and searching of heart; and one night shortly afterwards a young man stood up at the close of a meeting and acknowledged that God had visited and saved his soul. Thus was the downcast missionary cheered and sustained.

He was stationed for a short period in the city of Aberdeen, and was afterwards employed to labour among the navvies above Banchory, Aberdeenshire, by Colonel Ramsay of Banchory Lodge, whose brief but bright Christian career was soon after brought to a close by what might be called a translation from earth to heaven—from his couch to a throne in glory. All this time he was evidently being schooled for greater usefulness; and it was after he returned to Dundee in 1864 that his labours were most signally owned of God.

Robert loved best to work for daily bread in some honest calling, and to spend his leisure in seeking the salvation of the lost. From this period until the day of his death, he was hardly an hour unoccupied. His strength was great and his powers of endurance marvellous. He had occasion often to rise to his work at four o'clock; and instead of taking rest in the evening, he would go out to address a meeting or to speak in the street. Sometimes he was so weary that on his way home to his meals he found it necessary to seat himself on some doorstep and rest. Yet no sooner had he taken his supper, than he went to his knees for half an hour; and then, Bible in hand, took his way out to the blessed work of winning souls. Often, although exhausted with the duties of the day, did he, with another like-minded, run all the way, some two miles, to Lochee, where he conducted services; and as they sped across fields with breathless haste, sinking to the knees in mud almost at every step, his companion was frequently well-nigh fainting ere they reached the place of meeting. And on returning home at a late hour, it was often not to rest; for, moved with compassion on the lost, he would lay himself down before the Lord and weep and pray a great part of the night. Reader, do you wonder at that? Think of the value of a soul; think of its eternal destiny—its heaven or its hell; think of its awful peril; think of God incarnate dying for its salvation; think of the glory of its recovery, involving as that does the thought, the love, and the effort of the Triune Jehovah. Think of these things, and marvel not at the man's self-denying labours, but rather wonder that every man, with

"Ransomed from Sin, and Death, and Hell"

written with blood by the finger of God upon his brow, does not burn his life and powers away in ceaseless labours for the salvation of that undying crowd standing even now within an inch of eternal perdition.

Do you ask me what he preached about? Well, he spoke often about eternity. And truly, amidst the rush and roar of time, and the deafening rattle of earthly vanities, and the mad confused cry of ten thousand voices shouting, "Great is Diana of the Ephesians; great is the world, and blessed are they that possess and enjoy it;" amidst all the crackle and noise of the devil's bonfire, it is not unnecessary that some stentorian voice of God-fearing earnestness ring out upon the heavy stifling air this one word, with its infinite meaning, ETERNITY! ETERNITY! Ho! man, woman, whither away? Know ye not that the present moment is big with destiny, and that even now your steps are verging on the eternal?

> Eternity! eternity!
> How long art thou, eternity!
> And yet to thee time hastes away,
> Like as the war-horse to the fray;
> Or, swift as couriers homeward go,
> Or ship to port, or shaft from bow.
>   Ponder, O man, eternity!
>
> Eternity! eternity!
> How long art thou, eternity!
> For e'en as on a perfect sphere
> End nor beginning can appear,
> E'en so, eternity, on thee
> Entrance nor exit can there be.
>   Ponder, O man, eternity!
>
> Eternity! eternity!
> How long art thou, eternity!
> A circle infinite art thou,
> Thy centre an eternal NOW:
> Never, we name thy outer bound;
> For never end therein is found.
>   Ponder, O man, eternity!
>
> Eternity! eternity!
> How long art thou, eternity!
> How terrible art thou in woe!
> How fair where joys for ever glow!
> God's goodness sheddeth gladness here,
> His justice there wakes bitter fear.
>   Ponder, O man, eternity!

Eternity! eternity!
How long art thou, eternity!
Lo! I, eternity, warn thee,
O man, that oft thou think on me;
The sinner's punishment and pain;
To them who love their God, rich gain.
PONDER, O MAN, ETERNITY!

According to the Word of God, our witness-bearer divided man's eternity into two, and testified of coming joy and coming woe. "What is the use of preaching about hell?" say some with scorn, not unmingled with the impatience of a secret dread. Fling that taunt in the Master's face, we might reply, and do not blame the servant for walking in the Master's steps. Do poor sinners run faster to hell because they are affectionately warned to "flee from the wrath to come"? There is no such thing as future punishment, said Satan to Eve; "ye shall not surely die," although you sin. That is the devil's gospel; but it meets its refutation a long way on this side of eternity, for many a sinner knows in his heart that sin is terribly killing in every act.

One of the frequent topics of our homely lay preacher's discourse was the new or second birth. He could not handle nice points like a scholar, but he could state the truth as it stands in the Word, and illustrate the great doctrine of regeneration by the Holy Ghost from his own experience. He dealt unsparing blows at Pharisaism, formalism, Christless morality, and all polishing of the old man. "What is the use," he would say, "of cleansing the outside of the platter, when the inside is filthy?" He continued:

You may whitewash an old falling house, but it is none the more secure. You may paint and rig out an old rotten ship, but your paint won't prevent it from going down in the first storm. It will not do, dear friends, to patch up our old hard hearts and try to get into heaven with a little extra French-polish. The whole

inner fabric of a man is rotten; and one of the best proofs of
his rottenness, perhaps, is his great conceit in thinking that he
will get into heaven without being born again. Ah! you say, very
wicked men and sinners like Bob Annan need a great change in
order to be saved; but people brought up in a Christian way, who
have never gone far astray, surely cannot be put upon the same
level as those. Tell me how many ways of salvation are there?
Just one. And if you are to be saved, the best and genteelest of
you must humble yourselves and come and enter by the same
door as poor Bob Annan, or any other poor sinner who has no
righteousness at all. You wonder at that. *"Marvel not that I said
unto thee, Ye must be born again!"* (John 3:7).

On the streets his grand theme was salvation. I question
if he ever spoke without bidding his hearers read what is
written on the red banner of the cross. Salvation from sin,
from all sin; salvation from the dreadful curse of a law broken
by all men; salvation from the giant power of the universal
heart-rooted love of sin, a power more gigantic and crushing
than all tyrannies combined; salvation from the greatest evils
of life, from cares, fears, remorse, and all heart plagues; salvation from death, the devil, and hell; salvation blood-bought
and doubly sweet because coming through the life, obedi-
ence, death, and resurrection of Jesus, Son of God and Son
of man; salvation free as the air we breathe, to be had for the
taking; salvation full as the whole "fullness of God;" salvation
at the present tick of time to all who believe, since *"now* is
the accepted time, and *now* is the day of salvation;" salvation
enjoyed on earth in "the peace that passeth all understanding," in "the joy that is unspeakable and full of glory," in "the
hope of eternal life," in a word, in all the grace of the indwell-
ing Spirit, and in all the blessedness of fellowship with the
Father and the Son; eternal salvation in that "glory, honour,
and immortality," the lustre of whose dim and distant beams
dazzles the eye of faith and fills the heart with a strange,

sweet homesickness; this manifold salvation, I say, worthy of the songs of angels and the eloquence of God, was the constant theme of the man who could truly say with Paul, "This is a faithful saying, and worthy of all acceptation, that Christ Jesus came into the world to save sinners, of whom I am chief" (1 Tim. 1:15).

Very tenderly and wisely did he deal with young enquirers. He took them always to the Word, his own experience of former anxiety standing him in good stead. "Look at this," he would say, as he turned to the text, "The blood of Jesus Christ his Son cleanseth *us* from ALL sin." "Did you ever notice the word 'ALL' here?" he would ask. "Ah, you imagined there were some sins of yours which the blood of Jesus Christ could not cleanse. What do you think now?" The effect of all this was sometimes striking enough, as not a few can testify who are now treading the path of life. He constantly laboured to bring out the difference between grace and works; and there is not a passage bearing on this fundamental point in the epistles to the Romans and Galatians which he has not marked in his Bible, or had not expounded in his own way at one time or another. And as he expatiated on his favourite topic, salvation by free grace, he would say, "It is all grace, my friends; grace from first to last; and that is a grand thing for you and me. Look yonder at the grace," he would say, as if he then saw it literally, "look at it gushing out of the side of Jesus. Dear souls, Christ's side was opened that poor sinners might look in and see His bowels of compassion towards them."

The last time I heard Robert preaching in the street was shortly before his death. He began by singing one of his favourite hymns, which, in case any of my readers do not know it, I will here give:

I'm a pilgrim and a stranger;
   Rough and thorny is the road,
Often in the midst of danger;
   But it leads to God.

Clouds and darkness oft distress me,
   Great and many are my foes,
Anxious cares and thoughts perplex me;
   But my Father knows.

Oh, how sweet is this assurance,
   'Midst the conflict and the strife;
Although sorrows past endurance
   Follow me through life!

Home in prospect still can cheer me,
   Yes, and give me sweet repose;
While I feel His presence near me,
   For my Father knows.

Yes, He sees and knows me daily;
   Watches over me in love;
Sends me help when foes assail me,
   Bids me look above.

Soon my journey will be ended,
   Life is drawing to a close;
I shall then be well attended,
   This my Father knows.

I shall then with joy behold Him,
   Face to face my Father see;
Fall with rapture and adore Him
   For His love to me

Nothing more shall then distress me
   In the land of sweet repose;
Jesus stands engaged to bless me,
   This my Father knows.

After singing, he lifted up his voice in prayer somewhat as follows: "O Father, we are come out here to ask Thy blessing, and speak to poor sinners about salvation. Give us Thy Holy Spirit, that we may speak and hear as for eternity. Fill our hearts with Thy love, and may we all feel it good to be here. Give us a word to speak to these precious souls. Oh, come and speak to poor perishing sinners Thyself, and tell them that Thou lovest them and that Thy heart is yearning over them. Oh, put forth Thy power! Awaken, awaken the sleepers; for, O Father, they do not see their danger; they do not care about their souls. Take the anxious ones by the hand and lead them to the cross, and let them see Jesus and His bleeding side. There are poor hungry ones; bring them into Thy house and feed them, for there is enough and to spare. And there are poor naked ones; take them in and put Christ's clothes upon them, and then they will not shiver any more. There are poor things trembling in the cold of this cold world; oh take them in and warm them at Thy fire! If they only felt Thy love they would be warm enough. Do not let the devil spoil our meeting. Let him not hinder us in any way. Take the prey out of his hands this night, and give us a blessed season, for Jesus' sake. Amen."

The subject of his discourse was *Peace with God:*

My dear friends, have you peace? "Oh yes," you say, "I hate quarrelling and I love to be on friendly terms with my neighbours." Very good; but what will peace with your fellow-creatures do for you when you stand at the bar of God? If all the world were your friends and stood up to plead for you, would they get you off if justice condemned you? Have you peace with God?

You say, "Well, I am not disturbed in my mind." Ay, I see, you have peace with yourself. Well, that is not a bad thing, provided it is a good peace. It is a terrible thing for a man to be at war with himself. It is not so bad to fight with the devil as to fight with one's self. Many a man falls out with himself and then commits suicide because he cannot stand that sort of fighting. But what sort of peace have you with yourself? If you are not at peace with God, your peace with yourself is a delusion. It is like mist that blinds the traveller who is advancing towards a precipice. "For when they shall say, peace and safety; then sudden destruction cometh upon them, as travail upon a woman with child; and they shall not escape" (1 Thess. 5:3).

Peace with God is the great thing. If you have that peace, God is your friend and you need not care who is with you or who is against you. If you have peace with God you will have peace with yourself, you will have peace in your conscience. Oh, how sweet it is to lie down and sleep at peace with God! It was this that made Paul and Silas sing in a dungeon at the hour of midnight. It was this peace that made the martyrs so brave that they went to death as if they were going to a marriage, and sang for joy in the midst of the flames. This peace would support and cheer you in affliction, and it is the softest and safest pillow for a dying bed. If you were to lay your weary soul on this pillow and die tonight, you would wake in the arms of Jesus. Truly, it is a peace that passeth all understanding. Will you have it?

How can we get it? Well, here it is, in the blood of the Lamb of God. Jesus is the Prince of Peace. He came from heaven to be the maker of the peace and the messenger of it. He "made peace through the blood of His cross," as we are told in Colossians 1:20. He bore the penalty for us; He died for us; He did all and suffered all, and justice says it is enough. And "God was in Christ reconciling the world to himself, not imputing unto men their trespasses." Now, if you lay hold on Jesus as your substitute and Saviour, you will be able to say, "Being justified by faith, we have peace with God through our Lord Jesus Christ" (Rom. 5:1).

Will you have this peace? Do not think you can have peace with God and your sins too. If you get reconciled to God you won't go on fighting against your best friend. The blood of Jesus that makes me a friend to God makes me a foe to sin. Ah! Perhaps you are trying to keep up a kind of peace by going to church or sitting at the Lord's table, or by thinking you are not worse than most, and not so bad as many. Dear souls, do not suffer Satan and your own foolish heart to impose upon you in that way, else you will perish. That patched up peace won't do. Any peace that is not based upon the finished work of the Lord Jesus is just peace with Satan, peace in a condemned state, and a peace that will land you in hell. Be persuaded, dear friends, to come to Christ this very hour, and He will be your peace. God waits to receive and forgive you and make a covenant of peace with you. Oh, why not be reconciled to Him now? Perhaps you do not see your need of peace. Well, may God the Holy Ghost open your eyes; for your case is sad enough, and might make us weep.

I left Robert speaking; and some of his hearers, I have reason to believe, were led by him, or rather by the Spirit through his instrumentality, on that very night, or one of the nights following, into the way of peace.

4

Sowing Beside all Waters

He that observeth the wind shall not sow; and he that regardeth the
clouds shall not reap (Ecclesiastes 11:4).

> Sow ye beside all waters,
>   Where the dew of heaven may fall;
> Ye shall reap if ye be not weary,
>   For the Spirit breathes o'er all.
> Sow though the thorns may wound thee,
>   *One* wore the thorns for thee;
> And though the cold world scorn thee,
>   Patient and hopeful be.

"KEEP religion in its own place," is the demand of many who do not like to be regarded as the enemies of religion. Yes, by all means let us keep religion in its own place. But where is religion's place? Let a child answer. Where is God? Everywhere. "Keep religion in its own place" is nothing more or less than this: Give God His own place.

"Keep religion in its own place" means, in the lips of many: Let us have as little of religion as possible. They wish to go to heaven upon the minimum of religion. Let us have no more prayer, no more godly fellowship, no more holiness, no more of Christ, than we can help.

"Keep religion in its own place." Well, religion's place is the chief place, else it is a poor religion. There is a difference of opinion on this point. Many say, let us have religion by all means; but then it must be contented with a secondary place.

First business, and then religion, says one. First pleasure, and then religion, says another. First myself, and then religion, says a third. The mind of God is different: "Thou shalt love the Lord thy God with all thy heart, and soul, and strength, and mind" (Luke 10:27).

Robert did not often apologize to his audience; but sometimes, as I find from certain notes, he defended street preaching in this way:

> We come out to speak to you because—
>
> 1. We tremble to think of your present unhappy condition as sinners. 'God is angry with the wicked every day' (Psa. 7:11).
>
> 2. We wish to prevent your future misery. "It is a fearful thing to fall into the hands of the living God" (Heb. 10:31).
>
> 3. We wish you to enjoy the pleasures of religion, both in this world and in the next. "Wisdom's ways are ways of pleasantness, and all her paths are peace" (Prov. 3:17).
>
> 4. We wish to see souls saved, because it is for the glory of God. "Glory to God in the highest, and on earth peace, good will toward men" (Luke 2:14).
>
> 5. We wish it for the good of others; for when once you are saved, you will be a blessing to your friends and others. "Come and hear, all ye that fear God, and I will declare what He hath done for my soul" (Psa. 66:16).
>
> 6. We do it for our own sakes; for it brings us great happiness to labour for the salvation of our fellow men. "In watering others we are watered ourselves" (Prov. 11:25).

He was ever ready to lend his hand, his heart, and his voice when good was to be done. If someone was drowning, he plunged into the water and risked his own life to rescue another. Poor starving creatures he has taken home, and shared with them his own humble meal. If he could induce a wretched prostitute to leave her ways, he would write letters and entail on himself any amount of care and trouble to secure, if possible, her recovery. For the good of body or soul of any fellow-creature he was ever prepared to deny himself. But his chief delight was to preach in the street. The poor souls whom no man cared for were his great care. For them he wept and prayed and spent himself. "God has given me a thirst for saving poor drunkards and harlots," said he; and truly it was a thirst, intense and blessed. And the drunkards and harlots gathered in crowds to hear him. Rough as was his voice and manner, the intense earnestness of the man, the fervour of his prayers, the tenderness of his heart gushing out in tears as he spoke of Jesus saving the chief of sinners, the disinterestedness of his labours, and the genuine warmth of his soul, attracted and won the esteem of the poor, ragged, pale-faced, ill-conditioned stragglers on life's highway, who seem to themselves, if not also to others, to be outside the pale of light, and purity, and hope. Annan was a man of great faith. He knew that the God who had opened his own eyes, and saved his own soul could save the worst of sinners.

Often you might have seen him, as I have seen him, stand up to pray and talk of Jesus and of heaven in one of our Dundee Wynds—the narrowest of lanes, where the light of day struggles all too unsuccessfully for admission, the only shred of God's heavens visible between the lofty houses being a mere line of blue, frequently darkened by clouds of smoke; and where for the most part the only vestiges of civilization you can descry besides the dark, dank walls are the fluttering rags drying overhead, a couple of drunkards swearing doubtful friendship in the gutter, and a few half-naked children—the forlorn hope of the den—in the unconquerable joyousness of infancy, out playing in spite of hunger and cold. Around the indefatigable seeker of straying souls gathers, at the sound of a hymn, a motley crowd of coal-heavers, shore-porters, loafers, do-nothings, fish-wives, begging women with ill-favoured babes in their arms, girls of the streets, and others that defy all description; and as they listen to the bluff, manly, kind-hearted preacher, his solemn utterances begin to tell upon consciences that have long slumbered, and his passionate appeals find a response in the tears that score many an unwashed face. Suddenly a policeman advances towards where the preacher stands upon a chair and commands him to stop and go elsewhere. This is done at the instance of some neighbouring dram-seller, who rightly judges that his craft is endangered by the preaching and the praying. The preacher is disheartened, and the tear is in his eye as he steps from his homely pulpit to go away. The poor people are all touched: some are angry, and others are weeping. "Ay, ay," says one, "we ken wha has dune this" (meaning the publican); "it 'il no pit naething inta his pouch, I'se warren' ye. Had it been a chiel singin' a sang at a door he wad a latten him stan' till eleven o'clock at nicht. But the guid man maun gang awa'; and we'll nae get a chance ava." "Na, na," says another, "that's aye the wye. They wud prosekeete Christ Himsel' if He cam doon the closs."[1]

When Robert was driven from one place, he quietly, though sometimes reluctantly, went to another. And many of the poor people went with him; for the very worst felt that he was more their friend than the publican. When the dram-sellers could not avail themselves of the police, they sometimes hired the blackguardism of the locality to hoot and pelt the preacher down. Their success, however, was only partial; for the courageous soldier of the cross refused to be defeated by soot and mud, by blasphemy and cruel mockery; and he returned again and again to the field, till he fell in the

---

1 Trans: "Yes, yes," says one, "we know who has done this" (meaning the publican); "it'll not put anything into his pouch, I'll warrant you. Had it been a man singing a song at a door he would have let him stand till eleven o'clock at night. But the good man must go away; and we'll not get a chance at all." "No, no," says another, "that's always the way. They would persecute Christ Himself if He came down the close."

arms of victory. Not long before his death he was ordered by the police to leave his preaching stand and return no more. "May I not speak at such a place?" he asked. "No." "Well then, in Helen Street, which is not a thoroughfare?" "No." "Well, I will go home and take my stand in my own house, and open the window and shout with all my might, and every soul in my neighbourhood at least will hear of salvation."

He addressed meetings every Sabbath morning at Fish Street, or Couttie's Wynd, or Tyndal's Wynd, and every Sabbath evening in the same places, or somewhere else in the town. During the interval of public worship he held prayer meetings. And frequently on every night for three or four successive weeks he was engaged in the same good work. He spoke in the open air all the year round, often standing to his knees in snow. One day, when the rain poured in torrents, and his Bible became so wet that he could not turn the leaves, one of his fellow-labourers counselled him to retire; but Robert only said, "Thank God, dear friends, it is not raining fire and brimstone," and went on with his address. At midnight on the 31st of December, 1866, just as the new year came in, an awful voice was heard in the centre of the town, warning the noisy revellers, as they paraded the streets, of coming judgment, and calling them to repentance. In thunder tones it was heard above the din of the crowded street, pealing forth its one solemn message, "Prepare to meet thy God" (Amos 4:12). It was the voice of Robert Annan standing in the snow. He seemed to many as one that mocked. Well, we shall see. What time conceals, eternity reveals.

This devoted man found many ways of being useful. Often on going to his work at an early hour he would write on the pavement passages of Scripture, such as, "What shall it profit a man if he gain the whole world and lose his own soul?" "Except a man be born again he cannot see the kingdom of God." "God so loved the world, that He gave His only begotten Son, that whosoever believeth in Him should not perish, but have everlasting life." "Believe on the Lord Jesus Christ, and thou shalt be saved." "Turn ye, turn ye; why will ye die?"

And sometimes his compassion for perishing men was such that he could not sleep, and he would rise to steep his soul in tears at the throne of grace, and afterwards steal out in the silence of the night to write upon the pavement, "Are you saved for eternity?" "GOD IS LOVE." Thus many had the gospel preached to them as they went to their work at early morn, and were met on the threshold of the day by a voice from heaven preaching from the very stones.

Limited as were his means, he managed always to give away many tracts and little books. "You might get your portrait taken for five shillings," said his wife to him one day. To which he replied with much feeling, "My dear Jeanie, I would to God I had five shillings to buy gospel tracts with for poor sinners." Often, however, was he supplied with tracts through the generosity of kind-hearted Mr. J. Melrose of Edinburgh who, along with the Brothers Paton of Tillicoultry, and the late lamented Henry Craigie of Falcon Hall, have done so much in sending forth, through the Colportage Society of Scotland, such works as *Memoir of McCheyne* at such a price as poor people could afford.[1]

On one occasion his wife remarked that his hat was a good deal broken by his holding it in his hand when speaking in the street, and suggested that he should try and get a new one. Robert smiled in his contentment and said, as he looked at the old hat, "It will do with me very well, Jeanie. What I want is not a good hat but a good heart. Let us not seek the world's braws. What I want is heaven's braws—the grace of

---

1   Andrew A. Bonar, *Memoir and Remains of the Rev. Robert Murray McCheyne, Minster of St Peter's Church, Dundee.* Dundee: W. Middleton & Co., 1844.

God—the grace of God, Jeanie; and to help others to get it."

About six months before his death, an opportunity was afforded him of bettering his worldly condition by removing to Glasgow; but he said, "No. God is blessing my poor endeavours here just now, and I will not go. Saving souls is better than making money." Immediately after this, a remarkable blessing attended his labours; his meetings were crowded, and not a few were awakened and brought to the Lord. So true is it that "them that honour Me I will honour" (1 Sam. 2:30).

Besides adopting unusual methods of doing good, Robert found time to write many letters with the same end in view. To one who trusted in his own righteousness, he wrote:

DEAR SOUL

I love you, and my prayer is that your heart may be broken by the power and love of Christ and His cross. Since I spoke to you, my heart has bled for you, and I resolved on my knees to write you. May God open your eyes to see Jesus as the Saviour! You say you do not need to be a new creature—that only wicked people need to be born again. Surely you do not know yourself, or you would not speak in that way. All the Bible saints saw themselves to be very vile. Isaiah, a holy man, says, "Woe is me! I am undone. I am a man of unclean liPsa." Job says, "Behold, I am vile." Paul says, "O wretched man that I am! Who shall deliver me from the body of this death?" Every saint feels himself to be a black, hell-deserving sinner; and the holier they grow, they see their sinfulness more and more, because they are growing in grace and getting clearer sights of the divine glory and of their own vile nature. My own experience is this: when the Lord by His Spirit shows Himself to my poor soul, I abhor myself, and at the same time I have a peace that passeth all understanding and rejoice with a joy unspeakable and full of glory. Have you ever seen the blood of Christ so as to break your heart on account of sin? If not, you are a child of wrath.

The letter goes on to show, at great length, and by many Scripture proofs, the utter insufficiency and worthlessness of works in the matter of justification, and the necessity of being born again.

To a family that made a profession of religion but lived in practical ungodliness, he thus writes:

65, Spittal, Old Aberdeen

MY DEAR FRIENDS

Before I left you I may have said things which appeared harsh, but I cannot retract a single sentence. My conscience is clear before God in the matter. You may think that you have lived amiable lives and do not need to be converted like openly-professed sinners; but unless you take the same position before God as a poor sinner deserving hell, heaven's door will be shut against you. The holiest men who have ever lived acknowledged their vileness and saw themselves even as beasts before God (Psa. 73:22). The nearer one lives to God the more clearly does he see his own sinfulness.

Listen to the words of the Lord Jesus (Mark 7:21-22): "Out of the heart of man proceed evil thoughts, adulteries, fornications, murders, thefts, covetousness," etc., etc. Read also Romans 3. Dear friends, unless you can say "Amen" to these truths, you are in a bad case. I long to see you saved. I have sometimes feared that your consciences have grown gospel-hardened, and that you are given up. I hope I am deceived. I hope you will yet be awakened to cry, "What must we do to be saved?" I am sure it would cheer my poor heart, and it would cheer the heart of Jesus infinitely more."

The letter ends with a most solemn appeal.

Robert, observing that some ministers of the gospel address their congregations as if they were all saved, was much grieved. To a minister he writes the following:

65, Spittal, Old Aberdeen

<small>Dear Friend in Jesus</small>

I hope you will not be offended at me for writing you this note. Ever since I left —— I have been troubled about you and the people over whom God has made you overseer, as I do think few of them have tasted that the Lord is gracious. You may think otherwise; but dear friend, before God I would say, "You will have to preach the gospel more faithfully." I do think you flatter your people. I have heard you say, "If there are any unconverted ones here," as if your people were all true Christians; whereas, had you said, "If there are any Christians here," it would have been a great deal nearer the mark. I know the people, and few of them can give a practical reason of their hope for eternity, although they can give you the theory of it. For instance, there is John —— and his wife, and ——, and your Deacon P ——, and old ——, and Mrs. C——, who is hardening her neck, and many more whom I know.

I have read the works of those men who have been most used of God in the salvation of souls, and I cannot find an "if" in their sermons where you put it. I heard a man of God, much blessed in the awakening of sinners, say, "I am determined, God helping me, that no unworthy communicant shall sit down at the Lord's table here, unless they are amongst those who would, if possible, deceive the very elect"—very black hypocrites these.

Dr. John Love of Glasgow points out the error of ministers that I speak of. You will find no such way of speaking in McCheyne's sermons. Whitefield, Wesley, Bunyan, Baxter, and many living preachers, owned of God above others, never preached as if the people were all converted. I do hope you will clear yourself of the blood of souls, and make a distinction between the clean and the unclean, as God has done by the apostles and prophets. It is fearful to think that sinners are flattered into hell by their ministers. God help you to clear yourself of that great sin. Oh to realize more and more the dreadful eternity to which sinners are going! Friend, friend, I ask you to think of your poor flock, lest some of them should rise and curse your ministry on the great day. Get your soul filled with compassion for sinners. Get your own soul steeped in the love of God, and get the burden of other souls laid upon you, and I am sure you won't flatter sinners as I have heard you do. Read Jer. 6:14; Isa. 22:4, and 56:10-11; Gal. 4:19; Acts 20:31. Faithful preaching would empty your church of Pharisees but would fill it with living Christians. May God greatly bless you.

I am yours in Jesus,
Robert Annan.

To a friend he writes:

MY DEAR ——

I hope —— has gone to a better world. I have seen some dying like lambs—no bands in their death—but alas! no evidence of grace. Many are trusting in morality. These will not enter at the strait gate themselves, and they hinder others. Mere professors abound here. They have Christ in one hand and the devil in the other. I cannot call them Christians; they are Satan's servants in Christ's livery. Profane men go to hell by the gate, but these professors steal into it by the postern. Oh, eternity! Eternity! Who would not make sure of salvation? That man is mad who does not. Taking chance for eternity is surely the greatest folly. God grant, my dear ——, your feet may be on the Rock. Rest not until with a good confidence you can say, Christ is mine and I am His. The Lord save dear ——. I fear the world is her idol. May the Spirit convince her and give her no rest till she find it in the blood of sprinkling! I have written to M—— about salvation, and also to E——; I wish I saw them rejoicing in the Lord. I wish to clear myself of their blood. The Lord has blessed me with faith to grasp the promise. He is my dearest Friend, my best Beloved. Oh the blessed Jesus! He has accepted me, and I have given myself all and whole to be at His service. May the Lord humble me and lift Himself up. I wish Him to be glorified and myself cast down—out of sight. Self keeps many a Christian from enjoying Christ as he ought to do. Cursed self! It keeps the Saviour's face from shining on the soul.

Dear ——, let Jesus be all; let nothing be in His way—no idols, no stumbling-block. Let Jesus have a clear course into your heart. The nearer a man lives to God's dear Son, the comelier is he in the eyes of God, and angels, and godly men, but the more unlovely to a wicked world. Dear ——, build your nest on the Rock of Ages, fast by the altar and the throne of God. Let Christ be your only desire. Care for nought but Him. Nothing else will satisfy the soul. Oh, what a portion He is! The fullness of the Godhead is ours. A glorious God is ours. The Saviour is ours. The Holy Ghost is ours. All things are ours. Away then with every idol.

Improve your talent, and speak faithfully to ——. Remember the doom of the slothful servant. When the householder went out to hire servants, he did not go merely to those who were full of head knowledge, but to those who were idle. Go to the vineyard and work for Jesus. The devil will try to keep you back; but resist him, and cry for strength.

Go and warn M——. I feel for her, and for —— and family. How strange that people should refuse to be happy. Jesus has made me happy—even me; and my name is ungodly Robert Annan. Many will tell you they have a belief in Christ; but the belief of the unconverted is different from the faith of a Christian, which is wrought by the Holy Spirit. We are bound to say to these careless people, Believe, etc.; and yet it is like giving medicine to one who is not sick. The sinner must first be convinced of his sin and danger; and then the balm of Jesus' blood will be sought for.

The Lord bless you and be with you.
Yours in Jesus,
Robert Annan.

To one who was trying to hold both with Christ and the world, he writes:

My dear ——
I trust you will not be offended at me speaking so faithfully to you about your soul. I have been watching for signs of grace

in you, but can see none. God forbid that I should be unchari-
table; but, you know, the Lord Jesus says a tree is known by its
fruits. Now, the things I have seen and heard concerning you
are inconsistent with the grace of God.

The Word of God tells us that they who are friends of the
world are enemies of God. "If any man love the world, the love
of the Father is not in him." "Thou shalt love the Lord thy God
with all thy heart." "No man can serve two masters: ye cannot
serve God and mammon." "Because thou art lukewarm, and
neither cold nor hot, I will spue thee out of my mouth" (Rev.
3:16).

"If God be God, serve Him. If Baal be God, serve him." A
divided heart God will never accept. Christ is like the woman
mentioned in 1 Kings 3:25. The whole child or no child. The
devil is like the other woman, who wanted the child halved.
He wants sinners to enjoy the pleasures of the world, and hold
Christ too; but that will never do. The Lion of Judah and the
lion of hell can never be yoked in the same chariot. The Word
of God says, "Come out from among them, and be ye separate,
saith the Lord, and touch not the unclean thing; and I will
receive you" (2 Cor. 6:17).

Men who set their affections on the earth have lean souls.
Their Christianity is doubtful. If they are Christians, they will
be punished by God for serving other gods. They will be saved so
as by fire. They will get a tasting of hell before they enter heaven.

I hear of professing Christians who spend six or seven hours
dancing or in singing foolish songs, and never spend an hour
with God in their closets. Shame on them! I would not give
a straw for their chance of heaven. They are lovers of pleasure
more than lovers of God. May the Lord open their eyes. The
Lord says that some fear Him and serve their own gods (2 Kings
17:41). These are not God's dear ones. Another set are described
in the Word: "And they come unto thee as the people cometh,
and they sit before thee as My people, and they hear thy words,
but they will not do them: for with their mouth they show
much love, but their heart goeth after their covetousness" (Ezek.
33:31). Dear ———, read these passages for yourself.

You are convinced but not converted. Oh, dear ——, at the peril of your soul get a true conversion. There may be many convictions and yet no conversion. Satan has a counterfeit grace for every genuine grace of the Spirit. Examine yourself. When a man leaves the service of Satan to serve Christ, he gets a new set of tools altogether, and a new set of pleasures—psalms and hymns and spiritual songs and holy joys; but the Bible never speaks of your comic and other foolish songs, and there is not a word about men and women dancing country dances and reels, or any such thing, except they were godless creatures like Herodias' daughter. Oh now, for your very life, have done with all such things as these, and get holiness to the Lord. And if once you are filled with the Spirit, you will have pleasures that will last for ever.

Yours in Jesus,
Robert Annan.

The person to whom he wrote the above acknowledged he was right, and sought the Lord with many tears, and evidence of true repentance.

Thus in many ways did he labour for the good of souls. In town and country; by night and by day; by addressing crowds and by speaking to individuals; at the noisy fair and by the quiet sick-bed; without fear or favour; by prayers and fastings, tears and watchings and burning words, self-denials and holy deeds and heroic self-sacrifices; by sufferings and reproaches, and mockery and shame; by seven years of a laborious and Christlike life, which was but one long prayer to God and one great effort for souls, did this faithful follower of Jesus spend himself, and "all for love, and nothing for reward."

And with what results, do you ask? Great results—results worthy of an angel's ambition: the conversion of sinners, the salvation of souls. One of his correspondents writes to tell him about those who had been converted through his instrumentality in a certain place. There is one whose "battles with the enemy are very severe," but "she is rich in faith." And there is M—— H——, who "is growing very fast in grace." A deep work of God is going on in old ——'s soul. K. S. "is quite happy" in the Lord. E. and W. "are holding on steadfast in the faith." "These are all your children in the faith, and there are many more here whom I don't know."

I may here give a few of the cases that have come under my own observation. F. M., a young man, was leaving a meeting one winter's night, when Robert laid his hand on his shoulder, saying, "Let us walk home together." F. M. knew what Annan would say to him, and wished to escape, but could not. "How is it with your soul?" said Robert. "Well enough," replied F. M. "And what is your reason for thinking you are saved?" was the next question. The young man could give no reason, and began to feel unhappy. Robert urged the necessity of having one's hope for eternity well grounded. They came to a well at which several women were refreshing themselves. Robert could not pass them, and turned aside to speak of Jesus and the living water. "Now," said F. M. to himself, "I will slip away from that troublesome fellow;" but an eagle eye was on him and he felt ashamed to sneak away. The conversation was resumed. "Do you ever pray?" "Yes." "What do you pray?" "I pray the Lord's prayer." "Do you ever pray for a clean heart?" "No, never." "Then you never saw your need of a new heart?" "No." Robert had now got in the thin end of the wedge and began to drive it home. The young man promised to go to his knees that night and pray for a new heart. But he did not so pray. He tried to sleep, but in vain. He rose at length to humble himself before God, and continued all night praying; in the morning his face was swollen with weeping. The next day, instead of going to work, he went to seek the man from whom but the previous night he had endeavoured to escape as from the plague. He found him at his daily employment near the shore. The result was the young man's conversion.

J. F., a young man, was invited to Robert's meeting. He went, and such was the power of the word that J. F. imagined the speaker had discovered all his sins and was addressing him personally. He was brought under deep conviction, and at first attempted to build up a righteousness upon his prayers and religious duties. Again Robert's word came with power and demolished his ill-grounded hope. His mental distress was extreme. One day Robert took from his pocket a letter which he had written, and asked J. F. if he thought the statements contained in it were true. True! J. F. had no doubt of it, for he did not suppose that his friend could write down lies. "Well," replied Annan, "it appears that you can believe my words, but you cannot give God credit for speaking the truth. God promises to forgive your sins and save you if you but trust Him, and you will not." In this way the man was convinced of the sin of unbelief, and ultimately was enabled to lay hold on the arm of Christ for salvation. J. F. is now a diligent and useful labourer in the vineyard of the Lord.

D. M., another young man who had been living without God and without hope, went to a meeting and was awakened. For a long time he sought the Lord, but without finding rest to his soul. One night he was in great distress. Robert said to him, "D ——, you are casting anchor in the ship's hold instead of throwing it overboard; you are seeking peace in your own heart instead of looking out to Christ for it." This helped him to see his error, and not long afterwards D. M. found peace in believing and is now an earnest worker in the service of Jesus.

A man one day violently assailed him for preaching in the street. Robert meekly bore the assault. The man went home, but could not sleep; and next morning he went and begged Robert to forgive him, saying that he could not go to his work until he had received forgiveness. Robert assured him that he had freely forgiven him, and exhorted him to seek forgiveness of his sins from God, urging on him to accept Christ at once as his Saviour. That man has been also brought to Christ.

Mrs. —— was one night awakened on hearing Robert tell the story of his conversion. She was in deep distress, and when he went on to speak of the way of salvation, she thought it was too simple and easy. One night not long afterwards she found the Saviour. Great was her joy. Her husband was enabled to enter into the ark that same night; and all the hours till morning, and all the day following, were spent in praising and glorifying God. "Keep on the hill-tap," said Robert to Mrs. ——, "as lang as ye can. Ye'll likely be doon i' the glen yet afore ye're hame."

It would be easy for the writer to multiply instances, for many were awakened through his instrumentality during the last six months of his life. For several months the work of God was carried on with great success, both in the open air and in a large unfurnished room kindly granted for the purpose by the proprietor. The room was called "the Whiskey Shop." Many were awakened in the meetings held there, and souls were born into the kingdom of God. One and another will tell you how they found the Lord one night in "the Whiskey Shop."

5

Wayfaring and Warfaring

Speak unto the children of Israel, that they go forward
(Exodus 14:15).
Ye shall therefore be holy, for I am holy (Leviticus 11:45).

Nearer, my God, to Thee,
Nearer to Thee!
E'en though it be a cross
That raiseth me;
Still all my song shall be—
Nearer, my God, to Thee! Nearer to Thee!

"What are you doing at present?" asked a man of his neighbour one day. "I am reading a book that has only two leaves," was the reply. "Then it won't take you long to read it." Months passed away and they met again. "Well, what are you doing now?" "Why, I am still reading my little book." "What! and only two leaves in it?" "Yes, a white leaf and a red one." "I don't understand you." "Well, the white leaf is the holiness of God, and the red leaf is the blood of Jesus Christ His Son. When I study the white leaf and see my sin in the light of God's holiness, I am glad to turn to the red leaf and rest my eye on the blood of Jesus. And when I realize the preciousness and efficacy of the Saviour's blood, I feel a longing for holiness and turn again to the white leaf. The little book will occupy me all my life, and I expect it will be my joyful meditation through all eternity."

59

How few of the people of God go straight forward in the path of growing holiness! There are some, however, who never seem to turn back or turn aside or even stand still. Wise and happy souls! The subject of this sketch was one of these. So thorough was the work of grace in his conversion that he appeared to have no inclination left to return to his old ways.

His former life he now utterly abhorred. With what bitterness of godly sorrow did he often bewail his madness and the dishonour he had done to God! And this feeling and habit of penitence deepened onward to the end of his life. Like Rowland Hill, he found repentance to be a useful, if not also an agreeable companion, and one that he should part with only at the gate of heaven. Often have I seen the tears gush from his eyes when the days of his folly came back to his remembrance. When wicked men flung his former deeds in his face, he went aside and humbled himself anew before his God; and when Satan began to taunt him with the memory of his sins, he turned the adversary's weapon against himself, saying, "If I have been valiant for thee, let me be equally valiant for Christ."

It may be truly said that he had now only two ideas: personal holiness and the saving of souls. These ideas in his ardent nature were flaming passions. He really lived for nothing else, so mightily did the power of God work in his soul. He had but two weapons: the Word of God and prayer. The Bible was never out of his hands when he had a moment's leisure, and he carried it with him wherever he went. Prayer was his delight—secret, persevering, and importunate prayer. The first thing he did on going home to his ordinary meals was to repair to his closet. Hours of fellowship with God was a small thing with him. Often was his meal untasted when he went away to his work; he had been eating other meat. Three successive nights of watching unto prayer was his frequent practice. He never went to bed on Saturday night; the

Sabbath always found him on his knees. And his business at the throne of grace was simply this—personal sanctification and the salvation of a perishing world.

In the course of his pilgrimage he passed through the Valley of Humiliation. Once, a terrible darkness fell upon his spirit. God revealed to him the desperate wickedness of his heart, and although he had been previously walking blamelessly and in the fear of the Lord, he saw in himself every conceivable sin. He was horrified, overwhelmed, and almost driven to despair. He began now to write himself down "a black hypocrite." Formerly he found hell in the Bible; now, he said, he found it in his heart. He thought he was "another Judas." "Here I am before God," he writes, "nothing, I fear, but a black hypocrite; my best works are filthy in his sight, and what can I say? I would still plead Christ's blood; I cry, Grace! Grace! Free, free sovereign grace! By that alone can such an one as I be saved. I long for holiness, I hunger for it, and yet my heart is in a state of fearful hardness." For three whole weeks he never went to bed, but prayed and fasted all that time, until even his iron constitution began to give way. He fought with Apollyon and gained the victory by free sovereign grace. The Sun of Righteousness shone anew upon his soul and more sweetly than ever before. "Blessed is the man," he writes, "who can realize the sweet assurance of Christ's love. Some of His people, I daresay, as they journey along, have at times many doubts (which they ought not to have) whether they are really Christ's. What joy will be theirs as they are met by Him at the gate of Paradise and clasped in the bosom of His love. I have often doubted my heart, but I cannot doubt His promise, 'Him that cometh to Me I will in no wise cast out.' His blessed face is always smiling through the lattice of His Word—His yea and amen promises. If I had ten thousand souls, I think I could rest them all on one promise. Oh, the blessed Jesus! who can fathom His bound-less compassion?"

After coming out of the fiery ordeal referred to, his growth in grace was marked and rapid. He grew gentle, quiet, and meek. He was tenderly affectionate, and his love often showed itself in tears. He was not less solemn, but more loving in his public addresses; and his self-denying labours became more incessant. Insult, contumely, scorn and blows he bore with singular meekness. When a man cast soot upon him whilst he was preaching in the street, he said, "Man, but for the grace of God I would have knocked you down; but I will pray for you." And he did it.

Two young men, brothers, waylaid him one dark night with the intention of doing him bodily harm; but his gentleness disarmed them and they became thenceforth his warmest friends. A drunkard was beating his wife, and the neighbours, fearing she would be killed, called in Robert, who rescued the woman. On this the brutal husband turned upon his wife's deliverer and dealt him several blows. "Give him up to the police," cried a score of voices. "No," said Robert, "I will not; I have a better way." He began to speak kindly to the man. "See," said the woman, as Robert returned only kind words for heavy blows, "see what the grace of God can do!"

A certain man fiercely attacked him one day in the presence of many people and cast in his teeth all his misdeeds. "It is all true," said he, "too true. But the Lord Jesus has saved me and He can save you too." He felt this cruel attack, and went into the house of a fellow Christian to rest himself. He told how he had been wounded, but said again with tears, "It is all true." Having refreshed himself with a drink of water, he retired to an adjoining room and was heard pleading fervently for the salvation of his malignant enemy. When he came out he was quite himself again.

His progress in grace was clearly seen in his remarkable superiority to the cares of this life. During his last years he did not appear to have a thought about worldly goods. No one could engage him in a conversation about such things. Having food and raiment he was therewith content, and he troubled himself not about tomorrow. His constant saying was, "I must be busy about my Master's work, for my time is short." Prayer was his resource in every time of straits. At the beginning of one winter he came home at night shivering with cold, and his wife remarked that his coat was growing bare and thin, and he would need a warmer one for his open-air preaching. "Well, Jeanie," said he, "we'll tell the Master about it; and maybe He will give me a new coat." That night as he knelt in prayer he did tell his Master about the cold weather and the new coat. Next day he received a letter from some unknown friend; the letter enclosed three pounds. Robert held up the money in his hands and thanked his gracious Master. The new coat was procured, and the brave soldier felt he was well-harnessed for the winter's campaign. It was the last coat he needed; he soon exchanged it for the shining robes of glory.

On another occasion his wife reminded him that everybody else was to have a holiday, and it was a pity they could not afford to take the children to the country for a single day. Robert looked at the children and at his wife, and his heart was touched. "Well," said he, "perhaps the Lord will send us the means and we'll get a day out." That night he laid the matter before his Heavenly Father, and next day a letter brought the necessary means. "See," says Robert in an exultant tone, "see what a good Master we serve! Jesus not only gives His servants a holiday, but He pays their expenses too." Out of the heaven-sent store he provided himself with a large supply of tracts, and enjoyed the holiday none the less that he seized the opportunity of doing good. In one house he found an aged woman who, to his kind inquiries about her soul, made reply that she had no fear of death because her minister had told her the other day that she had nothing to fear for eternity, seeing she had been a well-behaved person and had always shown an obliging disposition towards her neighbours. Robert endeavoured to show her the utter worthlessness of her own righteousness as a ground of hope before God, and then poured forth a fervent prayer for her salvation. She burst into tears and said she had never heard such a man, and turning to the rest of the company, expressed her astonishment that they "hadna made a minister o' him."

Long had he prayed and panted for holiness; and surely of that holiness which distinguished the Lord Jesus, compassion for sinners was one great element. This Christlike feature marked him in no common degree. Towards the end of his life he could hardly pass any one without affectionately pressing upon their attention the things of eternity. At the latest hour of the night he would linger behind his companions to speak to thoughtless ones in the street. Coming home one night with his friend, he stopped to speak to four youthful wanderers in High Street. "Come away," said his friend. "Don't you see it is within five minutes of twelve o'clock? and you are quite exhausted." "Oh, let me speak to them! Poor souls, I must speak to them." He spoke to them; and they fairly broke down as he pleaded with them, weeping and entreating them to repent and turn to the Lord. He came away saying, "I have left them in the Lord's hands."

This was his ordinary course: speaking to man for Christ, and speaking to Christ for man. And this, instead of retarding his growth in grace, promoted his personal holiness in a remarkable degree.

6

The Last Week on Earth

And he said, I beseech Thee, show me Thy glory (Exodus 33:18).

> I stand upon the mount of God,
>   With sunlight in my soul;
> I hear the storms in vales beneath,
>   I hear the thunder roll.
>
> But I am calm with Thee, my God,
>   Beneath these glorious skies;
> And to the height on which I stand,
>   No storms nor clouds can rise.

On Wednesday, 24th July, 1867, just seven days before Robert Annan went home, he was standing upon a raft, and as he floated about he was suddenly visited with an extraordinary manifestation of God to his soul. He had long ere this attained to close, habitual, and almost unbroken fellowship with his great Redeemer; but now he was brought so near that for the time he knew not that he was in the body. The heavens seemed to open to his view. The glory of the Lord filled his soul with a radiance well-nigh insupportable. His cup was full. So near did Jesus come that he felt as if he were talking to Him face to face. So glorious did the Lord appear in His majesty that Robert bowed his head with awe; and yet so ineffable was the love and condescension of that peerless One, that His disciple was filled with a strange overpowering joy. How long this lasted he could hardly tell;

but the shaking of the raft upon the water reminded him that he was still outside of heaven. Robert spoke of this to his Christian friends and said, "Jesus came to me on the water, and I thought I was home." He looked upon this blessed experience as his Master's call to go home. "Do not wonder," he said to some of his brethren, "if you hear some strange thing about me one of these days."

This joy appears to have continued in a great measure with him until he finished his course. It was like Elijah's double meal in the wilderness, and in the strength of it he went even till he reached the mount of God. Near the very spot where he saw the glory of the Lord upon the raft, and seven days after, Jesus met him again, and Robert passed triumphantly through the waters to the joys of heaven and the bosom of his God.

Of such sublime joys we may say, these are the things that make a man willing to die—nay more, that make death blessed. But there are those who will call this mere fanaticism. Well, we would not give such fanaticism in exchange for their cold philosophy. The fanaticism that inspires a pure, unselfish life and leads to a noble, heroic, Christlike death is surely as valuable at least as the poor philosophy that lives only for itself and dies for nobody.

At this time, Robert had been instrumental in rescuing from death, if not also from a worse fate, a young woman who had wandered from the paths of virtue. He found her at an early hour of the morning near the docks, where she purposed to drown herself. For this class he had almost unbounded compassion, and he constantly sought their recovery. In company with a friend, he would walk up and down the streets at a late hour in the hope of saving some of them. A few days before he was taken away he was employed in that way, when a wretched creature accosted him, saying, "Here's a saxpence,

Bob; come and get a dram." Robert turned and gave her such a pitying look that the poor woman burst into tears.

On the Friday preceding his death, he, along with a Christian friend, took the girl whom he had found at the docks and sent her by train to a quiet retreat where, under the wing of a devoted Christian lady, she could find opportunity and incentives to enter on the path of welldoing. "Oh, how much I have felt and prayed for that girl!" said he. "I have cried for her like a child." Two days afterwards he wrote her the following letter—the last he ever penned:

Dundee, 28th July, 1867

My dear Friend

I write you this day about Jesus, the Saviour of poor sinners like you and me. I do not see any reason why you should not be washed in His blood, but that which every other careless sinner has.

You have cost me more tears than many. I trust not in these for any good to you, but I do trust in Jesus that He will save you.

Remember, dear Elizabeth, that more are praying for you than me, or even your dear mother, brother, or others. Jesus is at the Father's right hand pleading for you; and the reason why you are not in hell, suffering the vengeance of eternal fire, is because Jesus pleads and says, "Spare it yet a little longer, till I shall dig about it and dung it."

Dear sister, what a dreadful hell yours will be if you go there! You will have to go forcing your way over a mother's prayers, tears, and warnings, your own profession once made, and the entreaties of others. Will not all this make hell hotter? An eternal hell! Elizabeth, think about that! Mercy offered now! Think about that! Jesus inviting you! Think of that! His loving arms open to receive you! Think about that! Elizabeth, I wish I could give you to Jesus. I will try to do it by faith. Will you not go to the dear loving Saviour who bled and died on Calvary to save sinners like you from hell? Dear soul, will you resist Him any longer? I am as certain as I write this note that He will save you if you will but trust in Him.

I ask you as a dear friend to go to Jesus, and He will forgive you, taking you to His bosom, where you will be safe for ever.

I am, your real friend,
Robert Annan.

All Saturday night Robert, as was his wont, spent in prayer. On Sabbath morning he called his family for worship at half past six. After that he went to the police authorities and obtained leave to hold one more meeting in Couttie's Wynd. A like-minded fellow-labourer meeting him, said, "I am afraid, Robert, they will put us off the streets altogether;" to which he replied, "I've got my ain place *ance mair*, but gang ye to the streets, Willy."

At Couttie's Wynd, on Sabbath morning, he began the meeting by singing:

> For ever with the Lord,
> Amen, so let it be;
> Life from the dead is in that word,
> 'Tis immortality.
>
> Here in the body pent,
> Absent from Him I roam,
> Yet nightly pitch my moving tent
> A day's march nearer home.

After prayer, he spoke from "Ichabod, the glory is departed" (1 Sam. 4:21). After fully stating the Scripture narrative, he said:

Dear friends, in the preaching of the gospel the ark of God has been brought to Couttie's Wynd, and you know that the idols have been falling before it. And if the gospel were allowed to have free course into your hearts and homes by the power of the Holy Spirit, it would sweep every idol away. But alas! Like the

Philistines of old, some of you are determined to send the ark of God away because it is proving too strong for your idols. Oh, consider what you are doing! You cannot have Christ and your idols too. What will your idols do for you at the hour of death and at the bar of the great God? Are you so mad as to prefer a lust, a little money, or drink, or ease, or pleasure, to Jesus and the salvation of your never-dying souls? God in His mercy prevent it! But it has come to this: will you have Christ and eternal life, or your sins and perish for ever and ever? Oh, how happy you would be if you only received Jesus into your hearts!

Dear children, I cannot tell you how happy I was last Wednesday morning down there upon the water when the Lord showed me His glory. If you but tasted these joys you would wonder at your present foolishness in putting Christ away from you. I may never have another opportunity of speaking to you. I may be in heaven before next Sabbath; and methinks I shall look down from glory on Couttie's Wynd. Oh, dear, dear souls, if you will not have Jesus and salvation—if you die in your sins—these walls will testify against you, for they have resounded with the offers of salvation made to you; this pavement will testify against you; and I will be a swift witness against you on that great day. "Oh, turn ye, turn ye; why will ye die?"

> Stop, poor sinner, stop and think,
>   Before you further go;
> Can you sport upon the brink
>   Of everlasting woe?

On returning from his morning service he went to church; but he was so filled with divine light and joy that he could not enter the sanctuary, and retired to pour out his soul in secret praises. In the afternoon he went and spoke to the gypsies, then encamped in the neighbourhood; came home and went to his knees again; then to Lilybank to address an open-air meeting; and again to Couttie's Wynd at seven o'clock. Thence again to the gypsies' tent, where he spoke, sang, and prayed. He returned to his own house at half past ten in a state of complete exhaustion but full of joy in the Lord.

Such was Robert Annan's last Sabbath on earth. His Sabbaths during the seven years of his life of faith had been spent in much the same way. And the last two days of his pilgrimage were occupied in his usual way—at his earthly calling during the day and at night in the Lord's vineyard.

7

Going Home

They that be wise shall shine as the brightness of the firmament; and they that turn many to righteousness as the stars for ever and ever (Daniel 12:3).

> From the far-off fields of earthly toil
>   A goodly host they come,
> And sounds of music are on the air—
>   'Tis the song of the Harvest-home.
> The weariness and the weeping,
>   The darkness, has all passed by,
> And a glorious sun has risen—
>   The sun of eternity.

The time was at hand when the Master's "Come up hither" should greet the servant's ear and be received with a joyful "Here am I." He had no fear of death; his faith had put every fear to flight. He had often prayed that God might be glorified in his death, and the prayer was about to be answered in a remarkable way. He felt assured that the Lord had granted that desire of his heart. One day, on leaving his closet to go and speak for Jesus at the fair, one of his relatives said: "It is of no use for you to go, Robert; they won't hear you." To which he replied with much solemnity, "Well, if they will not hear me whilst I live, I am persuaded God will make them hear Him by my death."

He had prayed for a triumphant death. One day, when speaking about heaven, Mrs. B. said, "I'll be satisfied if I manage somehow to get in." "What!" said Robert, pointing to a sunken vessel that had just been dragged up the Tay, "would you like to be pulled into heaven by two tugs like the London yonder? I tell you, I should like to go in with all my sails set and colours flying."

He had worked hard and lived fast in the Master's service. He had done more in seven years than many in seven times seven. "You are working too hard, Robert," was often said to him. His reply was, "The harder I work I'll get the sooner hame. We must deny ourselves; we'll no get to heaven on a feather bed." On the morning of Wednesday, July 31st, he rose at four o'clock and spent a long season in secret prayer. Some of the neighbours heard the sound of his wrestlings and remarked to his wife that Robert had been "very busy with his God that morning." He returned to breakfast as usual, and after family worship spent half an hour in secret prayer. He then hung upon the outside walls of his house two boards, on which were pasted the following placard, issued by Mr. Duncan Matheson, editor of the *Herald of Mercy*, a periodical blessed of God to the conversion of many souls:

THE
TWO ROADS

## THE BROAD	## THE NARROW
Its Gate is wide (Matt. 7:13)	Its Gate is strait (Matt. 7:14)
Its way is dark (Prov. 2:13)	Its way is light (John 8:12)
Its paths are false (Prov. 14:12)	Its paths are truth (Psa. 25:10)
It is crowded by those who forsake God (Isa. 1:4)	It is trod by those who forsake sin (1 Peter 3:10-11)
Who do iniquity (Isa. 59:3)	Who do the will of God (Matt. 7:21)
Who serve the devil (John 8:44)	Who serve the Lord Christ (Col. 3:24)
It Leads to Misery (Rom. 2: 9)	It Leads to Happiness (Psa. 64:10)
Death (Rom. 6:21)	Life (Matt. 7:14)
Judgment (Matt. 12:36)	Eternal Glory (1 Peter 5:10)
Its end is HELL, where there is wailing and gnashing of teeth (Matt. 8:42)	Its end is HEAVEN, where there is fullness of joy and pleasures for evermore (Psa. 16:11)

READER

MARK! ON THIS SIDE YOU HAVE	AND ON THIS SIDE YOU FIND
DEATH!	LIFE!
DAMNATION!	SALVATION!
SATAN!	GOD!

Along which of these roads are you hastening?—for in one or the other you most certainly are. Are you on the way to GOD and HEAVEN, or SATAN and HELL? A mistake, if continued to the end, will be fatal! "For what shall it profit a man if he shall gain the whole world, and lose his own soul?" (Mark 8:36).

Jesus Christ says, "I am the Way, the Truth, and the Life: no man cometh unto the FATHER BUT BY ME" (John 14:6). "He that believeth on Me hath everlasting life" (John 6:47). "Him that cometh to Me I will in no wise cast out" (John 6:37). "I came not to call the righteous, but sinners to repentance" (Mark 2:17). "The Son of Man has come to seek and to save that which was lost" (Luke 19:10).

WHERE WILL YOU SPEND ETERNITY?

"The current proved too strong for even the strong swimmer, and two boats were put off to his assistance."

He then took a piece of chalk and wrote upon the pavement "ETERNITY," and on the gate "DEATH," and went to his work at the docks. In two hours he met Death, to him in Christ a vanquished foe, and entered Eternity, to be for ever with the Lord.

He was, as we have said before, a powerful swimmer. "Swimming," he said, "was a gift bestowed on him by God, and he desired to use it for the glory of God." The first life he saved was that of his brother Ebenezer. When boys they were one day bathing. Ebenezer could not swim, and going beyond his depth began to sink. Robert, alarmed by his cry, swam to the spot and dragged him to the shore. In the course of a few years in the latter part of his life he had saved at least six or seven lives. In one day he saved two. After having rescued the first of these he went home, and putting on a good suit of clothes, he said with a smile, "I should not like to jump in again and spoil my good clothes, and yet I don't think I could resist the temptation." On returning to the harbour he heard the cry raised that another boy was drowning, and instantly plunging in, good clothes and all, he plucked the youth from the jaws of death. One boy whom he was saving he held up in the water, and all the while spoke to him of Jesus, saying, "Trust in Jesus, He will save you from eternal death."

Some time previously he had been presented with the Dundee Humane Society's silver medal, and the resolution of the society printed on parchment, in acknowledgment of his heroic efforts. Such things as these he did not despise; but he could not overlook the greater value of the soul's life, and he had ever an eye to the final recompence of reward. Once, when presented with several volumes by those to whom he had been the messenger of Christ, he said, "I would much rather, dear friends, that you would help me to bring more souls to Jesus." When his wife expressed a fear that he would one day lose his life in saving others, he replied, "Dear Jeanie,

could I look on a fellow-creature perishing and not endeav-
our to save him?"

To return to our narrative. About twelve o'clock a boy,
eleven years old, fell into the water, and Robert, hearing the
cry, plunged in to save him. Having reached the spot where
the boy was struggling for life, he laid hold on him, and
bidding him "hang on by his neck," he made way for the
shore. But the current proved too strong for even the strong
swimmer, and two boats put off to his assistance. The child
was saved, but the man of God went down. He might have
saved himself by letting the boy go, but he did not do so. The
self-sacrificing and Christlike man would save another if he
perished himself. Waving his hand, as if bidding farewell—so
says a spectator of the scene—and with a smile on his face,
he laid himself on his back and went down. Down, did I say?
No, not down, but up! For the man himself, the nobler part,
washed in the blood of Christ and clad in the beauty of holiness, went up to be for ever with his God.

Some taunt the followers of Jesus with being weak and
mean. Was Robert Annan such a one? A braver, a manlier
fellow never lived. How few live as he lived during his last
seven years! How few could die as he died! He died for
another. He gave his life for the life of a poor boy whom he
had never seen before.

He died in his thirty-third year, in his prime, and in the
midst of his usefulness, as we in our short-sightedness are
wont to say; but let us not forget that the Lord takes His
people home not merely because their work is done on earth,
but because they are needed in heaven. This, perhaps, is one of
the things we know not now but which we shall know here-
after. When Robert Annan lay across the railway all night in
America, God mercifully preserved him when no human aid
was near; but now, when many were at hand to help, the Lord
took him. In the former case he was ripe for destruction and

the Lord interposed to save him from temporal and eternal death; but now, when he was ripe for glory, neither his own strength nor the strength of others could keep him one hour longer away from his Father's house.

When the waters closed over him as a shroud, the angel-guard was ready to carry him aloft and the bells of heaven pealed forth his welcome home. What a sight met his enraptured spirit! Now his eyes behold the King in his beauty; his feet tread the gold-paved streets of the New Jerusalem. He shines as a jewel in Immanuel's glorious diadem. No tear shall ever dim his eye again, for the hands that were nailed to the cross have wiped them all away. Amongst the ransomed company his voice may be heard joining in the song—never ending and ever new: "Unto Him that loved us, and washed us from our sins in His own blood, and hath made us kings and priests unto God and His Father; to Him be glory and dominion for ever and ever. Amen."

ETERNITY

IN MEMORIAM.

By desire of Hon. James Gordon, the word eternity— that word which impressed Annan so deeply—was graven on the pavement before Annan's door.

8

Unexpected Echoes

Devout men carried Stephen to his burial
and made great lamentation over him (Acts 8:2).

A voice is heard on earth of kinsfolk weeping
    The loss of one they love:
But he has gone where the redeemed are keeping
    A festival above.

The mourners throng the streets, and from the steeple
    The funeral bell tolls slow;
But on the golden streets the holy people
    Are passing to and fro,

And saying, as they meet, "Rejoice! Another,
    Long waited for, is come;
The Saviour's heart is glad—a younger brother
    Hath reached the Father's home."

The death of Robert Annan was felt to be a public calamity. Thousands wept for him as if each had lost a brother or a friend. Groups of working men stood at the corners of streets discussing the sad event; and as they talked, many a brave man turned away to hide his tears. In the east end of Dundee you would have thought there was one dead in every house. "I question," it was said, "if ever there was so much weeping in this town for one man." Seldom, indeed, has such been the case. The man who but a few days before his death was despised and hated by many—who was mobbed, derided,

79

hooted down, pelted with soot and stones, and spat upon, for the sole crime of preaching Jesus to perishing men— was now the object of universal lamentation! Ten thousand tongues spoke of him only in terms of praise. Newspapers[1] and religious periodicals carried the thrilling story of his life, conversion, heroic labours and death to hundreds of thousands throughout the land, and many that were melted by the touching recital heard at the same time what the grace of God can do. This was surely an unexpected echo. Was it not the voice of God in answer to Robert's prayer that his death might be the occasion of blessing to the people of his native town?

On Saturday, the 3rd of August, the remains of this faithful soldier of the Cross were buried in the Eastern Necropolis. The funeral was in every respect of an extraordinary character. The great bell of the old steeple rang out a solemn peal—an honour, it is said, accorded to a working man for the first time in the present century. This was done by order of the Provost, and met with universal approval. A vast multitude, thoughtful and sad, assembled near the house where the dead lay; and many pressed in to take a "farewell look of the brave and laborious hero" whose "manly and massive features looked much as he had been often seen—mourning for sinners. Many brave men faltered beside that coffin. Never in the halls of kings did tears fall more fast and freely than those that fell in the 'but and ben' which was the humble but happy home of Robert Annan."[2] A short service was then conducted. Besides the reading of the 90th Psalm, and the offering of prayer, a hymn which Robert had often wished his friends would sing in his dying hour was read and partly

---

1   A thrilling sketch, from the pen of Mr. James Scrymgeour, appeared in the *Dundee Advertiser* and the *Herald of Mercy*. It touched the hearts of thousands.

2   A 'but and ben' is a two-room cottage.

sung. The hymn, which well expresses his faith, his heavenly-mindedness, and his full assurance of hope, is as follows:

> Come sing to me of heaven
> 　When I'm about to die;
> Sing songs of holy ecstasy,
> 　To waft my soul on high.
>
> When cold and sluggish drops
> 　Roll off my marble brow,
> Break forth in songs of joyfulness,
> 　Let heaven begin below.
>
> When the last moments come,
> 　Oh, watch my dying face,
> To catch the bright, seraphic glow
> 　Which on each feature plays!
>
> Then to my enraptured ear
> 　Let one sweet song be given;
> Let Jesus cheer me last on earth,
> 　And greet me first in heaven.
>
> Then close my sightless eyes,
> 　And lay me down to rest,
> And clasp my cold and icy hands
> 　Upon my lifeless breast.
>
> When round my senseless clay
> 　Assemble those I love,
> Then sing of heaven, delightful heaven,
> 　My glorious home above.
>
> 　There'll be no more sorrow there,
> 　　There'll be no more sorrow there.
> 　In heaven above, where all is love,
> 　　There'll be no more sorrow there.

It may well be believed that the singing proved too much for human nature, and that the whole company were bathed in tears. Prayer was again offered out of doors, the minister standing on the stone on which was still legible, as written by Robert on the morning of his death, the word "ETERNITY." Some six hundred men, among whom was the chief magistrate, marched behind the hearse to the place of burial. Great crowds of spectators, many of them deeply affected, lined the streets; and numbers of women, dressed in mourning, followed the procession to the grave, weeping as they went. There again a portion of Scripture was read and prayer offered; and as the clods were falling upon the coffin lid, a thousand voices broke out singing, with thrilling effect:

> My Jesus, I love Thee, I know Thou art mine,
> For Thee all the pleasures of sin I resign;
> My gracious Redeemer, my Saviour, art Thou,
> If ever I loved Thee, my Jesus, 'tis now.
>
> I love Thee, because Thou hast first loved me,
> And purchased my pardon on Calvary's tree;
> I love Thee for wearing the thorns on Thy brow,
> If ever I loved Thee, my Jesus, 'tis now.
>
> I will love Thee in life, I will love Thee in death,
> And praise Thee as long as Thou lendest me breath;
> And say, when the death-dew lies cold on my brow,
> "If ever I loved Thee, my Jesus, 'tis now."
>
> In mansions of glory, and endless delight,
> I'll ever adore Thee in the heaven of light;
> I'll sing with the glittering crown on my brow,
> "If ever I loved Thee, my Jesus, 'tis now."

Thus again was heard an unexpected echo. What meant all that homage to a plain working man? It was doubtless the Master calling for a testimony to the worth of His servant. The testimony was freely and touchingly given. "The righteous shall be in everlasting remembrance" (Psa. 112:6).

On the Sabbath following, a funeral sermon was preached in Hilltown Free Church—the church of which he was a member. The attendance was so great as to render it necessary to conduct the service in a neighbouring field. Nearly three thousand were present. The text was Gen. 5:24, "And Enoch walked with God: and he was not; for God took him." At the close of the discourse the preacher, after describing Annan's conversion, spoke as follows:

His decision of character is worthy of note. He was naturally warm of temperament and resolute of will; impulsive, vehement, and impetuous. On his conversion, all this force of character was consecrated to the service of God. In his praying, he seemed to be taking the kingdom of heaven by violence; and in his preaching you would have thought that, brooking no denial, he would then and there have all his hearers accept of offered grace. His spirituality was deep-toned and genuine. He studied the Word of God incessantly; his Bible was his constant companion. He spent much of his time in prayer; long watches of the night often passed whilst he tarried at the mercy seat, pleading not only for himself but for others.

When special services were being held in the church or in the town, Robert would sometimes spend a whole night alone with God. His zeal was a steady flame. His love to men's souls was intensely fervent. Especially did he pity and care for those for whom no man cared. "I know not how it is," he said to me, "but I feel a constant hunger and thirst for saving poor drunkards and harlots."

He had strong faith, and never seemed to despair of the recovery of the worst. His courage was never daunted. I do not think he ever knew fear. He did not weary in welldoing. His efforts for the good of others were in a great degree self-denying. Almost every night, and several times every Sabbath, he would go out to speak or pray somewhere. Often last winter did he stand with the snow to his knees, and with streaming eyes plead with men to turn to the Lord and live. Instead of resting after his day's toil, he would go away out to the exhausting but delightful work of seeking to save the lost. Whilst thus employed he did not neglect other duties.

He was a faithful servant, an obliging neighbour, and he cared for his family's welfare. Sometimes he spoke to me with tears about his little children. I have gone to his house and found him with his Bible on one knee and his babe on the other. He was helping his wife. When wearied beyond measure, he would lie down with the cradle string in his hand, resting himself whilst he rocked the child. His progress in the Christian life was constant and marked. He longed to be holy. Once when I took occasion to point out what I deemed an error, he thanked me with tears in his eyes, and warmly grasping my hand, said, "That is the very thing that has been hindering my growth in grace."

His usefulness was great. He will be missed by many. "There is nobody now to care for my soul," said a poor woman, as she wept and looked on the dead body of this remarkable man. Not a few attribute their conversion to his instrumentality. He died the death of a hero. He lost his life in saving the life of another.

Farewell, brave spirit. Another light is quenched on earth; another star shines in glory. Another voice is hushed in the church below; another voice now joins in the song above. There is one servant of God fewer on earth; there is one more to serve in heaven. Farewell, brave soul. We shall meet again. Till time is done, and the heavens be no more, my brother, I bid thee farewell.

Throughout the service the deepest solemnity prevailed; and when at the close the preacher referred to the much-missed brother, now absent from the body but present with the Lord, the vast assembly gave way to emotion—strong men weeping in silence, while many of the women sobbed aloud. It was a memorable day; and as there was more than mere natural feeling at work, the results have doubtless been more permanent than emotion, and more precious even than tears.

What was all this but the echo of that manly voice which had so often proclaimed salvation in the cold streets and pled for sinners at the midnight hour?

It was suggested that a fund should be raised by public subscription for the relief of his widow and orphans. Through the instrumentality of several gentlemen well known in this town, whose efforts were beyond all praise, and backed by the influence of the *Dundee Advertiser*, the fund speedily became, under God's blessing, a great success. Money poured in from all quarters, town and country, from wealthy men and working men alike—the latter having formed an "Annan Fund Committee." One of the first to bring his subscription was a man who had often abused Robert while preaching; his liberality and his tears now told another tale. Many of the poor, for whose welfare he had so lovingly toiled, brought their contributions also—some, indeed, all the money they had in the world. The amount quickly rose to five hundred pounds. This surely was the finger of God. Robert Annan had sought no earthly recompense; but his gracious Master threw the arms of His lovingkindness around the orphans and the widow, and proved the truth of His own Word, "Leave thy fatherless children, I will preserve them alive; and let thy widows trust in Me" (Jer. 49:11).

The impressions made by his death were numerous, varied, and deep. One man was found lying on the grave and weeping. "I have been a very wicked man," he said, "but the grace of God, perhaps, will do for me what it did for Robert Annan. Noble Robert Annan! I wish I were like you." Couttie's Wynd was a Bochim. Several were awakened, and some who had been halting between two opinions took up the cross and began to follow Jesus. A girl of the street, who had heard him preach on the last Sabbath of his life, came crying and saying, "Oh, I canna get rest; I canna get rest! I think I hear him yet. The wa' o' the hoose is cryin' oot against me, as he said it wud do; an' the very stanes o' the street are aye condemnin' me. Oh, what'll I do? what'll I do?"

Many of the godly were stirred up to seek greater devotedness to the Lord and loftier attainments in grace. Some who till this time had been idlers in the vineyard have begun to work for Christ; whilst those who had been toiling amidst many discouragements have been incited to greater boldness and zeal. An impulse has thus been given to evangelistic effort; and as the result, souls have been added to the Lord. It appears that our Christian hero has, like Samson, accomplished more by his death than by all the labours of his life. Such were some of the echoes of his departing steps, as he passed from earth to heaven—idlers in the vineyard stirred up to work, faithful labourers incited to double their diligence, slumbering formalists startled, careless sinners arrested, waverers brought to decision, and souls saved. Results such as these are surely worth dying for; more blessed echoes no saint of God could ever wish to leave behind him.

Reader, you see how much may be accomplished by a single talent faithfully employed. Of learning, Robert Annan had none; gifts of intellect were not his; of eloquence he knew nothing; wealth, influence, office, or commanding position never fell to his lot. One talent, however, he certainly possessed, and that was an indomitable will. He refused to be driven from his purpose; difficulties only stimulated his spirit to more energetic action, and he was not to be turned aside either by cowardly fears or worldly bribes. A resolute will, sanctified by the Spirit, sustained by prayer, and guided by a single eye, was the basis of his Christian character, the spring of his courage, his zeal, and his perseverance, and the secret under God of his power and success. He walked so closely with God that he could hardly have failed of great usefulness. Writing to a young man who was studying with a view to the ministry, he says:

If God's servants are to be useful, they must be holy and devoted to the work. God will not honour unholy men in the ministry. Oh to be single-eyed in the Master's service! Oh to seek the glory of God and not the praise of men! To have a childlike trust in the faithfulness of our heavenly Father! To live near, yea, to lean on the very bosom of Jesus and be filled with His Spirit! Then shall we be instrumental in saving souls, and then shall we be able to smile at the taunts and frowns of an ungodly world.

By means of his one talent, his single eye, and unceasing prayer, he was made a blessing to all classes of people. One night he met a professing Christian who lacked assurance. Robert did not leave him until he was filled with the joy of the Spirit's testimony to his sonship. Another night, as he returned from a meeting, he hailed a company of believers. "Are you all saved?" was his question. They replied in the affirmative. His searching glance fell upon them, and he asked with great solemnity, "Dear friends, are you all saved for eternity?" More slowly came the second reply, "We believe we are." "Well," said Robert, "give all the glory to God," and then passed on. There was something awe-inspiring in his manner; and that little knot of believers dispersed to their several homes and to their closets to examine themselves and give diligence to make their calling and election sure. Men, his superiors in intellect, education, and position were not ashamed to take a leaf out of his book. A minister of the gospel in a certain parish where Robert had conducted a series of successful meetings was awakened by the zeal of the simple evangelist and immediately began to preach and pray and labour for the good of souls as he had never done before. On meeting any of his flock, instead of discoursing on worldly topics as formerly, he began to say, "How is it with your precious soul?" The people were all amazed, the godly were delighted, and the results, it cannot be doubted, will be lasting as eternity.

Christian Reader, have you only one talent? Be encouraged. Lay it on the mercy seat beside the blood; plead incessantly for the power to employ it faithfully, and you shall not live in vain. So did Robert Annan. "Go thou and do likewise."

One thing is written, as with a sunbeam, on the life of this man—it is this: the grace of God can save the chief of sinners. How was it that he who, in the wantonness of mischief, had more than once felled a man like an ox, learnt to repay cursing and blows with blessing and kindness? How was it that he who in Canada was prevented from committing murder by the immediate interposition of Divine Providence became so loving and so insatiable in his desires for doing good that he often said, "I think I could not live unless I now and then saw some sinners brought to Jesus"? How came it to pass that he who had revelled in all manner of grossest sin, and had in his desperate wickedness laboured to obliterate from his heart the last trace of belief in a Divine Being, became so pure and holy that his highest ambition was to be like Jesus, and his supreme happiness lay in communion with God? What is the explanation of that change from infidelity to faith, from cruelty to mercy, from hatred to love, and from utter depravity to holiness? The answer is plain: he was born again. On the night on which he was awakened, he rushed into the house, where but a few days previously he had stoutly and with scorn denied the doctrine of regeneration by the Holy Ghost, and exclaimed, "Tell me about the new birth. I see now I must be born again if I am to be saved. Oh, what a hard heart I have! Nothing will melt it." He sought and obtained the fulfilment of this gracious promise, "Then will I sprinkle clean water upon you, and ye shall be clean: from all your filthiness, and from all your idols, will I cleanse you. A new heart also will I give you, and a new spirit will I put within you: and I will take away the stony heart out of your flesh, and I will give you an heart of flesh. And I will put My Spirit within you, and cause you to walk in My statutes, and ye shall keep My judgments, and do them." (Ezek. 36:25–27.)

It is hardly necessary to remark that Robert Annan was not without faults. Sometimes in his manner he was blunt to rudeness, stern to harshness, and hasty to impatience. His roughness, however, fitted him for the rough work his Master gave him to do; and his faults were those of a straightforward and thoroughly honest man. None who knew him could conceive his doing a mean action, or in any circumstances telling a lie. His faults grew less and less to the close of his life, till at length a singular sweetness and gentleness characterized his spirit and manner. We need not marvel at his remarkable growth in grace when we reflect that the keynote of his Christian life is found in the following extract, pasted on the flyleaf of his well-worn Bible:

> I will therefore just name a few of those things which every true Christian can safely pray for: the knowledge of our complete acceptance in Jesus; a more decided growth in grace; increase of holiness; greater spirituality of mind; more devotedness to God; stronger faith in His Word; more habitual reliance upon Christ for all things; a spirit of grace and supplication; a conscience increasingly tender; a greater regard for God's glory than our own advantage; a more grateful heart for our numerous unmerited mercies; the enjoyment of every new covenant blessing; a more growing hatred to sin and more steady resistance of it even in its first approaches; to be enabled to bear a more decided testimony before the world of the truth and importance of religion, and furnish clearer evidence of our being the children and servants of God.

Reader, are you born again? Are you washed in the blood of Jesus? If not, why not now? Once, when Robert Annan preached at Aboyne, a young man, trembling with alarm, came up and acknowledged that he was not saved. "Then," said the faithful evangelist, "if you die as you are, you will drop into hell." "True, true," was the young man's reply. "Well then, flee to the Refuge; you may die tonight." But he resisted the strivings of the Holy Ghost and went away, saying, "Oh, surely I won't die so soon!" In a few days, without any apparent change, he was called to meet God at the judgment bar, and now his state is fixed, and that for ever!

"Procrastination," said a great preacher, "is the recruiting officer of hell." Reader, "Now is the accepted time; behold, now is the day of salvation."

> Return, O wanderer, to thy home,
>   Thy Father calls for thee;
> No longer now an exile roam
>   In guilt and misery.
>
> Return, O wanderer, to thy home,
>   'Tis Jesus calls for thee;
> The Spirit and the Bride say, Come!
>   Oh, now for refuge flee!
>
> Return, O wanderer, to thy home,
>   'Tis madness to delay;
> There are no pardons in the tomb,
>   And brief is mercy's day.

Appendix

A friend deeply interested in the work of God, in which he had taken an active part during the years 1859–60, had the following printed for very extensive circulation. Robert Annan made large use of it, and God blessed it to precious souls. Much fruit has since been gathered in Dundee and through the land. What was written then is equally fitted for today.

PLAIN WORDS FROM A FRIEND

My dear Fellow-Sinner

You have heard of the Revival and about the wonderful things which the great God did for us in Scotland some time ago. Many have reviled God's blessed work, and I wish to tell you something of the truth about it.

You know that many people come from the church the same as they go to it; the Word does not touch their consciences, and they remain under the power of sin and Satan—of death and hell! This used to be very much the way among us until lately; but the God of love visited us and poured out His life-giving Spirit upon the dead souls of men.

In some places you might see the solemn sight of hundreds weeping for their sins and seeking to give up their hearts to Jesus. And ah, what a sweet change has taken place in many! The high looks of the proud have been brought down; dead formalists have become living Christians; worshippers of mammon have been changed into lovers of God; the blasphemous tongues of the profane have been made to sing God's praise; drunkards have cast from them the cup of devils, and have taken the cup of salvation; unclean persons, who used to be the slaves of lust, and the very dregs of humankind, are now sitting at the feet of Jesus; and some who were ringleaders in every form of sin are now bold and open and unflinching in the service of Christ, even as they once were shameless and hard-hearted in the service of the wicked one. Many who formerly were dead in sin are now living in the grace of Jesus, in the love of God, in the communion of the Spirit, and in the hope of heaven!

Dear fellow-sinner, do you not think that you need such a change as this? And do you not think that all our towns and villages and parishes stand in need of such a glorious work of God among their perishing thousands?

I am sure you must see that if the Bible be true, the multitudes everywhere are on the highway to hell. Many are fighting for wealth as if they had an eternal lease of life. Many are as proud as if they were not heirs of wrath. Multitudes follow Satan blindly and are murdered for eternity. Multitudes take the name of the Lord God in vain. Multitudes crowd into the tippling-houses, which are Satan's shambles, the open mouths of hell!

Young men and young women, think of it! Tippling-house keepers, think of it, and give back your license; or, if you are still resolved to retail for the devil, oh, write, for the sake of miserable souls, above your doors, "A SHORT ROAD TO THE PIT."

How many stagger along to the pit! How many wait and walk about to see if Satan will buy their souls for a lewd companion! Ah, Satan is quick to strike so good a bargain! He often buys souls cheap; and never more so than on the Sabbath, when multitudes seek their own pleasure, forgetting that God has said, "REMEMBER THE SABBATH DAY TO KEEP IT HOLY."

Sinner! Is this state of things to continue? It cannot continue. Mercy or judgment must end it. The land is ripe for Christ's atoning blood or for God's devouring wrath. Sinners must repent and be saved or go on and be damned. There is no middle ground to stand upon. The blood of Jesus and the power of the Holy Ghost are the only refuge. To these turn at once, while God waiteth to be gracious and putteth a drag upon the wheels of vengeance. And oh, beware of delusive remedies.

There is one remedy, and there is one only: the blood of God's only begotten Son, and the almighty power of the Holy Ghost. The blood of Immanuel can cleanse a world from its iniquity; it can wash this Sodom-like land and make the blackest sinner in it whiter than the snow. The Spirit of the Lord is not straitened. A nation shall yet be born again by His power in one day. He can awaken the consciences of thousands and cause them to cry out as one man, "Woe is me! I am undone!" "Lord, save me; I perish."

Such things England, Scotland, and Ireland have already seen; and perhaps the time may come when God shall by His Spirit work so gloriously that Satan shall be driven from his throne in the land and millions shall rejoice in God's salvation.

Fellow-sinner, it is time to seek the Lord! Who shall say it is not? Oh, blinded sinner, can you stand in the piercing flames of wrath? Can you find the fire of hell a downy bed? Can you meet Jehovah when the great day of His wrath is come? Awake from your sleep; it is a sleep on the edge of a precipice! Turn to God now. Come out of the Satan-bound multitude; cast yourself at the feet of Jesus; receive the Holy Ghost.

God is now waiting to be gracious; but if you refuse His love, you must endure His wrath; if you reject Jesus as a Saviour, you must meet Him as a Judge; if you will not submit to Him and follow Him to heaven, you must submit to Him at last and be driven from His blessed presence into the company of devils and the damned!

Oh, dear sinner, will God's love not move you? Will the wounds and blood of God's own Son not break your heart? Yield, oh yield to God, and be saved! "Come, Holy Ghost, descend in love upon this sinner's soul, cast out Satan, and bring him to the feet of Jesus." Amen.

I have spoken plainly, as I would not be charged with the blood of souls; and praying for your salvation,

I am, dear fellow-sinner,
YOUR SINCERE FRIEND

Verily, verily, I say unto thee, Except a man be born again, he cannot see the kingdom of God.

The "eternity stone" as photographed by Charles and Mona Leiter in the summer of 1988

Eternity

EXTRACTED FROM *THE HERALD OF MERCY!*
A MONTHLY MAGAZINE

Those who have read the life of Robert Annan, the Christian hero, will remember that just before he met his death, he wrote in chalk on the stone before his door the word ETERNITY. The Hon. James Gordon, second son of the late Earl of Aberdeen, caused those letters to be cut in the stone, and we now present our readers with an engraving, showing the gate of Robert Annan's house and the word on the stone. There it lies before the eyes of every passer-by, a reminder that time will not last for ever.

By and by the traffic of countless feet will wear that stone away; every day the word will become fainter and fainter, till no trace is left.

But time that wears the stone away brings eternity near. Are you prepared for the great change that awaits you? The state you are in when death finds you will be the state in which you will continue throughout eternity. Heaven or hell; there are but two places. Christ or Satan; there are but two rulers—Christ in heaven, and Satan in hell—each ruling over his own subjects.

"I am the Door," said Christ; "by Me if any man enter in he shall be saved." Will you not enter in before the door is shut? What will it profit you to gain the whole world and lose your own soul? If you gain Christ you gain everything. Choose ye this day. Remember Eternity!

Also from Kingsley Press:

With Mercy and With Judgment
by Alexander Whyte

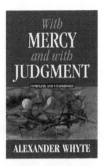

Harold St. John, a great Bible teacher and preacher of a previous generation, was once asked which commentaries and helps to Bible study he would recommend. His reply went something like this: "A man who deals with Scripture," he said, "has a conscience which needs to be trained, a heart which must be warmed, and a will that should be yielded, and finally, a mind which must be fed. For the conscience, none is better than Alexander Whyte—his *Lord, Teach Us to Pray* and *With Mercy and With Judgment* will make his readers hot and ashamed." And sometimes, being hot and ashamed is just what we need, spiritually speaking. "Do no put off reading Whyte's sermons," urges Warren Wiersbe in his *50 People Every Christian Should Know.*

The sermons found in this collection were deemed by the compilers to be representative of Dr. Whyte's pulpit ministry. The title was taken from the hymn which was mostly closely associated with his ministry, being the one he chose perhaps oftener than any other for the close of a service.

Dr. Alexander Whyte (1836-1921) was widely acknowledged to be the greatest Scottish preacher of his day. He was the minister of the largest and most influential congregation in the Free Church of Scotland. He was a mighty pulpit orator who thundered against sin, awakened the consciences of his hearers, and then gently led them to the Savior. His "pulpit presence" or force of personality was said to be almost as powerful as his preaching, which very often focused on the wrath of God against sin and His mercy toward sinners. He was also a great teacher, who would teach a class of around five hundred young men after the Sunday night service, instructing them in the way of the Lord more perfectly. He also served as professor of New Testament literature and principal of New College, Edinburgh. His many books include: *Bible Characters, Commentary on the Shorter Catechism, The Duty of Prayer, The Apostle Paul,* and many others.

Lord, Teach Us to Pray

By Alexander Whyte

Dr. Alexander Whyte (1836-1921) was widely acknowledged to be the greatest Scottish preacher of his day. He was a mighty pulpit orator who thundered against sin, awakening the consciences of his hearers, and then gently leading them to the Savior. He was also a great teacher, who would teach a class of around 500 young men after Sunday night service, instructing them in the way of the Lord more perfectly.

In the later part of Dr. Whyte's ministry, one of his pet topics was prayer. Luke 11:1 was a favorite text and was often used in conjunction with another text as the basis for his sermons on this subject. The sermons printed here represent only a few of the many delivered. But each one is deeply instructive, powerful and convicting.

Nobody else could have preached these sermons; after much reading and re-reading of them that remains the most vivid impression. There can be few more strongly personal documents in the whole literature of the pulpit. . . . When all is said, there is something here that defies analysis—something titanic, something colossal, which makes ordinary preaching seem to lie a long way below such heights as gave the vision in these words, such forces as shaped their appeal. We are driven back on the mystery of a great soul, dealt with in God's secret ways and given more than the ordinary measure of endowment and grace. His hearers have often wondered at his sustained intensity; as Dr. Joseph Parker once wrote of him: "many would have announced the chaining of Satan for a thousand years with less expenditure of vital force" than Dr. Whyte gave to the mere announcing of a hymn. —*From the Preface*

Buy online at our website: **www.KingsleyPress.com**
Also available as an eBook for Kindle, Nook and iBooks.

GIPSY SMITH
HIS LIFE AND WORK

This autobiography of Gipsy Smith (1860-1947) tells the fascinating story of how God's amazing grace reached down into the life of a poor, uneducated gipsy boy and sent him singing and preaching all over Britain and America until he became a household name in many parts and influenced the lives of millions for Christ. He was born and raised in a gipsy tent to parents who made a living selling baskets, 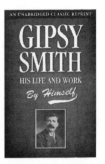 tinware and clothes pegs. His father was in and out of jail for various offences, but was gloriously converted during an evangelistic meeting. His mother died when he was only five years old.

Converted at the age of sixteen, Gipsy taught himself to read and write and began to practice preaching. His beautiful singing voice earned him the nickname "the singing gipsy boy," as he sang hymns to the people he met. At age seventeen he became an evangelist with the Christian Mission (which became the Salvation Army) and began to attract large crowds. Leaving the Salvation Army in 1882, he became an itinerant evangelist working with a variety of organizations. It is said that he never had a meeting without conversions. He was a born orator. One of the Boston papers described him as "the greatest of his kind on earth, a spiritual phenomenon, an intellectual prodigy and a musical and oratorical paragon."

His autobiography is full of anedotes and stories from his preaching experiences in many different places. It's a book you won't want to put down until you're finished!

THE AWAKENING
By Marie Monsen

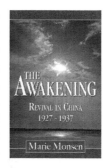

REVIVAL! It was a long time coming. For twenty long years Marie Monsen prayed for revival in China. She had heard reports of how God's Spirit was being poured out in abundance in other countries, particularly in nearby Korea; so she began praying for funds to be able to travel there in order to bring back some of the glowing coals to her own mission field. But that was not God's way. The still, small voice of God seemed to whisper, "What is happening in Korea can happen in China if you will pay the price in prayer." Marie Monsen took up the challenge and gave her solemn promise: "Then I will pray until I receive."

The Awakening is Miss Monsen's own vivid account of the revival that came in answer to prayer. Leslie Lyall calls her the "pioneer" of the revival movement—the handmaiden upon whom the Spirit was first poured out. He writes: "Her surgical skill in exposing the sins hidden within the Church and lurking behind the smiling exterior of many a trusted Christian—even many a trusted Christian leader—and her quiet insistence on a clear-cut experience of the new birth set the pattern for others to follow."

The emphasis in these pages is on the place given to prayer both before and during the revival, as well as on the necessity of self-emptying, confession, and repentance in order to make way for the infilling of the Spirit.

One of the best ways to stir ourselves up to pray for revival in our own generation is to read the accounts of past awakenings, such as those found in the pages of this book. Surely God is looking for those in every generation who will solemnly take up the challenge and say, with Marie Monsen, "I will pray until I receive."

Buy online at our website: **www.KingsleyPress.com**
Also available as an eBook for Kindle, Nook and iBooks.

A Present Help
By Marie Monsen

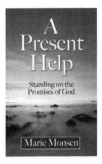

Does your faith in the God of the impossible need reviving? Do you think that stories of walls of fire and hosts of guardian angels protecting God's children are only for Bible times? Then you should read the amazing accounts in this book of how God and His unseen armies protected and guided Marie Monsen, a Norwegian missionary to China, as she traveled through bandit-ridden territory spreading the Gospel of Jesus Christ and standing on the promises of God. You will be amazed as she tells of an invading army of looters who ravaged a whole city, yet were not allowed to come near her mission compound because of angels standing sentry over it. Your heart will thrill as she tells of being held captive on a ship for twenty-three days by pirates whom God did not allow to harm her, but instead were compelled to listen to her message of a loving Savior who died for their sin. As you read the many stories in this small volume your faith will be strengthened by the realization that our God is a living God who can still bring protection and peace in the midst of the storms of distress, confusion and terror—a very present help in trouble.

Buy online at our website: **www.KingsleyPress.com**
Also available as an eBook for Kindle, Nook and iBooks.

ANTHONY NORRIS GROVES
SAINT AND PIONEER
by G. H. Lang

Although his name is little known in Christian cirl-
ces today, Anthony Norris Groves (1795-1853) was,
according to the writer of this book, one of the most
influential men of the nineteenth century. He was
what might be termed a spiritual pioneer, forging a
path through unfamiliar territory in order that others might follow. One of those who followed him
was George Müller, known to the world as one who
in his lifetime cared for over ten thousand orphans
without any appeal for human aid, instead trusting

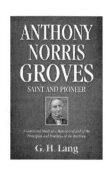

God alone to provide for the daily needs of this large enterprise.

In 1825 Groves wrote a booklet called *Christian Devotedness* in
which he encouraged fellow believers and especially Christian workers to
take literally Jesus' command not to lay up treasures on earth, but rather
to give away their savings and possessions toward the spread of the gospel
and to embark on a life of faith in God alone for the necessaries of life.
Groves himself took this step of faith: he gave away his fortune, left his
lucrative dental practice in England, and went to Baghdad to establish
the first Protestant mission to Arabic-speaking Muslims. His going was
not in connection with any church denomination or missionary society,
as he sought to rely on God alone for needed finances. He later went to
India also.

His approach to missions was to simplify the task of churches and
missions by returning to the methods of Christ and His apostles, and to
help indigenous converts form their own churches without dependence
on foreign support. His ideas were considered radical at the time but later
became widely accepted in evangelical circles.

Groves was a leading figure in the early days of what Robert Govett
would later call the mightiest movement of the Spirit of God since Pen-
tecost—a movement that became known simply as the Brethren. In this
book G. H. Lang combines a study of the life and influence of Anthony
Norris Groves with a survey of the original principles and practices of the
Brethren movement.

MEMOIRS OF DAVID STONER

EDITED BY WILLIAM DAWSON & JOHN HANNAH

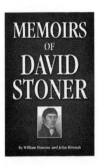

The name of David Stoner (1794-1826) deserves to be ranked alongside those of Robert Murray McCheyne, David Brainerd and Henry Martyn. Like them, he died at a relatively young age; and like them, his life was marked by a profound hunger and thirst for God and intense passion for souls. Stoner was saved at twelve years of age and from that point until his untimely death twenty years later his soul was continually on full stretch for God.

This book tells the story of his short but amazing life: his godly upgringing, his radical conversion, his call to preach, his amazing success as a Wesleyan Methodist preacher, his patience in tribulation and sickness, and his glorious departure to be with Christ forever. Many pages are devoted to extracts from his personal diary which give an amazing glimpse into the heart of one whose desires were all aflame for more of God.

Oswald J. Smith, in his soul-stirring book, *The Revival We Need,* wrote the following: "Have been reading the diary of David Stoner. How I thank God for it! He is another Brainerd. Have been much helped, but how ashamed and humble I feel as I read it! Oh, how he thirsted and searched after God! How he agonized and travailed! And he died at 32."

You, too can be much helped in your spiritual life as you study the life of this youthful saint of a past generation.

"Be instant and constant in prayer. Study, books, eloquence, fine sermons are all nothing without prayer. Prayer brings the Spirit, the life, the power." —*David Stoner*

The Way of the Cross
by J. Gregory Mantle

"**D**YING to self is the *one only way* to life in God," writes Dr. Mantle in this classic work on the cross. "The end of self is the one condition of the promised blessing, and he that is not willing to die to things sinful, *yea, and to things lawful*, if they come between the spirit and God, cannot enter that world of light and joy and peace, provided on this side of heaven's gates, where thoughts and wishes, words and 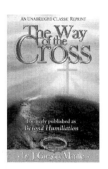 works, delivered from the perverting power of self—revolve round Jesus Christ, as the planets revolve around the central sun....

"It is a law of dynamics that two objects cannot occupy the same space at the same time, and if we are ignorant of the crucifixion of the self-life as an experimental experience, we cannot be filled with the Holy Spirit. 'If thy heart,' says Arndt in his *True Christianity*, 'be full of the world, there will be no room for the Spirit of God to enter; for where the one is the other cannot be.' If, on the contrary, we have endorsed our Saviour's work as the destroyer of the works of the devil, and have claimed to the full the benefits of His death and risen life, what hinders the complete and abiding possession of our being by the Holy Spirit but our unbelief?"

Rev. J. Gregory Mantle (1853 - 1925) had a wide and varied ministry in Great Britain, America, and around the world. For many years he was the well-loved Superintendent of the flourishing Central Hall in Deptford, England, as well as a popular speaker at Keswick and other large conventions for the deepening of spiritual life. He spent the last twelve years of his life in America, where he was associated with Dr. A. B. Simpson and the Christian and Missionary Alliance. He traveled extensively, holding missions and conventions all over the States. He was an avid supporter of foreign missions throughout his entire career. He also edited a missionary paper, and wrote several books.

Made in the USA
San Bernardino, CA
22 November 2013